A
SECOND
CHANCE

Surviving Sudden Cardiac Death

A SECOND CHANCE

Surviving Sudden Cardiac Death

Patrick W. Emmett

Bascom Hill Publishing Group
212 3rd Avenue North, Suite 570
Minneapolis, MN 55401
612-455-2293
www.bascomhillpublishing.com

ISBN - 978-1-935098-03-4
ISBN - 1-935098-03-9
LCCN - 2001012345

Book sales for North America and international:
Itasca Books, 3501 Highway 100 South, Suite220
Minneapolis, MN 55416
Phone: 952.345.4488 (toll free 1.800.901.3480)
Fax: 952.920.0541; email to orders@itascabooks.com

Cover Design by Jennifer Rumbach
Typeset by Peggy LeTrent

Printed in the United States of America

Table of Contents

Dedication

I dedicate this book to the four angels who rescued me on that cold January day in Minnesota:

Nancy, Kevin, Wendy, and David.

I also would like to offer special thanks to my three amigos, the entire hospital staff at Abbott Northwestern Hospital in Minneapolis; my cardiologist, Dr. James Harbrect, and my family physician, Dr. Steven Broxterman.

Special thanks to Dr. Janis Amatuzio for your encouragement and advice on bringing this book to the public.

Foreword

I suffered a heart attack while traveling on a business trip that quickly led to a Sudden Cardiac Arrest (SCA) and death. I died on an airplane that day and was brought back to life by the quick thinking and intervention of some wonderful and caring people. My story, however, is about so much more. My story is one that tells of the dramatic chain of events that led up to my SCA and the many changes I've had to face since that day. I've also had to cope with the simple fact that I had survived death. This may sound simple enough…you'd think that after death, the survival part would be easy, but survival is not as easy as one would think.

I am not a physician. I am a survivor. I wrote this book in an effort to connect with other survivors and other people who want to know more about heart health and who may have experienced similar life-changing events.

The book is intended to help save lives through the education of readers about Sudden Cardiac Death. Through the book I also want to recognize the many medical professionals and emergency first responders who are faced with death every day and rarely have the opportunity the see the net results of their efforts in the lives of those they have saved.

I will also delve into the "after death" experience and relay many of the stories that Sudden Cardiac Death survivors have shared with me about what happened after they died. These experiences are a haunting reminder that we are only here for a short while. The reality is that we could do a better job of taking care of ourselves and those we love.

Finally, this book is a guide for better living and coping with a heart condition. Many books provide excellent medical advice about why you should eat better and exercise more often. However, this book expounds on these simple truths from the perspective of one who's actually attempted to follow doctor-recommended guidelines. I am living proof of the value of their tried-and-true advice.

This book is a chronicle of my own story and the many dramatic circumstances of my post survival struggle. I have been fortunate to meet some wonderful people along the way, both in the medical profession, as well as other people who have survived their own Sudden Cardiac Arrest. All of them have touched me in a very special way. They are all very much a part of my survival.

If I can encourage one person to change his or her lifestyle, convince even one person to help place an AED in a public place, a parent to test their child for genetically related heart conditions or for you, the reader, to go in for a complete blood test and analysis so the net effect will be to save at least one life, then these words will have done what they were intended to do.

I owe my survival to the efforts of many people. In fact, there is no way to adequately express my appreciation to everyone who has experienced my pain and worked hard for my recovery. At times, I felt like the guy in the cell phone commercial accompanied by an ever-present network wherever he goes. Everyone was there for me, equally concerned for my well-being. This is such an enormous concept to grasp. We, as human beings, are really on this earth for the purpose of offering a helping hand to one another as chance and opportunity present themselves.

1

My Story

If I can stop one heart from breaking,
I shall not live in vain.
If I can ease one life the aching,
Or cool the pain,
Or help one fainting robin,
Into his nest again,
I shall not live in vain.
—Emily Dickinson

"A hero is an ordinary person who performs an extraordinary act under outrageous conditions." Someone once used that definition and I couldn't agree more. What I'm about to share is a story of heroes…a story of those who performed amazing feats, exhibited courage, and offered unconditional love…a story of those who displayed professionalism, yet whose hearts shone through. In many ways, this story is not my own. You may recognize some of these heroes from your own story.

Monday, January 23, 2006

I got up at 5:15 that morning, in order to catch an early flight. Because I travel quite a bit for work, I am all too familiar with the morning chaos at the airport. That morning I knew the drive to the airport would be both lengthy and tedious. Then, of course, I had to park my car, catch a shuttle to my gate, check my bags, and hope I got a decent seat placement. I was there early to allow extra time for everything to fall into place for my day. This particular morning, I was in line for security scanning and had my boarding pass an hour-and-a-half ahead of my scheduled departure. I took a quick inventory of everything I needed for my business trip and felt confident my trip would be successful.

I had just received a new computer bag as a gift from my wife for my business trips. This wasn't any ordinary computer bag. I could fit not only my computer but also my printer, my presentation materials, and all of the wires and hook-ups I would need. I could even stuff a novel into the front pocket of my case to occupy any uneventful minutes during my trip. I had a terrific computer bag that was heavy. I was fully prepared for my trip, but not for what I experienced that day.

I cleared security at the airport and settled into a seat to work on my computer. Kansas City International had free Internet access, so I was able to catch up on my e-mail. Time flew by as I worked, until I checked my watch. Time was getting dangerously close to departure and they had not yet called the flight. A rush of anxiety surged through me, since I still had a connection to make in Minneapolis. I was concerned that I might have a real tight connection.

Hoping for answers, I got in line and ask the gate agent what was going on. He explained that there had been a flight delay and that an announcement was pending. Although I appreciated his willingness to hear me out, I knew that my connection in Minneapolis could be threatened by the delay. The friendly gate agent checked the monitor and, sure enough, the next flight out of Minneapolis would be later that afternoon. If I flew on a later flight, I was worried that I wouldn't have enough time to complete my work before I had to leave again.

I wasn't happy, but there was nothing I could do. I fretted over the time and went back to my computer work. Airlines generally allow for a certain amount of flight delay in the connection time between flights, so I decided to assume everything would work out.

I was traveling that day on a Northwest Airlines flight from Kansas City to Sioux Falls, South Dakota. Once in Sioux Falls, a rental car would be waiting for me for my drive to the impressive city of Mitchell, South Dakota. Mitchell is famous for the Corn Palace, a building that's decorated with multi-colored corncobs replicating ornate depictions of people and historical events each year. The Corn Palace is really quite a sight and is the community's pride and joy. My agenda included a meeting with a car dealer to study and analyze his parts and service departments. If my efforts were successful I would be able to provide additional training for the dealership personnel. The analysis would be quite time consuming and I planned to get started as soon as I arrived.

Annoyed at the ticking minutes, I tapped my watch to see if perhaps the minute hand was moving forward. I was already an hour past departure time, practically guaranteeing my missed connection flight in Minneapolis. Finally, the announcement came and we boarded. I got an excellent seat and I remember thinking, *Ah…my luck is changing.*

I read my book all the way to Minneapolis. When I exited my seat, I was near the front of the plane, so I was able to de-plane quickly. I headed for the bank of departure monitors on the wall. I checked my watch and learned that I had twenty minutes before my next flight. Quickly, I scanned the monitors looking for Sioux Falls–I found the listing and did a double take. I had come into gate G-8. The departure for Sioux Falls was at gate A-2. I had to find an airport map—and fast. A-2 was on the opposite side of the airport. I took off fast for a very long walk—or should I say jog—and then a train ride to get there. I made a rushed "two-step" while using the moving sidewalks and then the train to get to gate A-2. I made the gate with five minutes to spare.

The ticket agent smiled warmly, as I handed my ticket to her. I wiped the beads of sweat from my forehead, and the agent's smiled waned. The ticket machine had rejected my ticket. Finally she said, "Oh! This ticket is for Sioux Falls. My gate is for Sioux City."

My heart sank. I knew I had missed my connection. The agent noticed my look of desperation and announced that she'd call over to the other gate to let them know they'd have a late arrival.

"You mean I might make the flight?" I queried.

"Yes, but you'll have to hurry."

I thanked her profusely and took off in a flash.

I dodged around people, skipped the train—because I saw that the train had just passed going the opposite direction. I then picked up the pace into a trot the whole way to gate F-6. You see, F comes before G and if I had just turned left, instead of right, I would have been at the gate with time to spare. As I rushed through the airport, cursing my stupidity, I kept thinking, "I'm not going to make it; I'm not going to make it."

I made it! My ticket was scanned and I was admitted onto the plane. Although I felt badly that I had detained everyone, my mood was lifted. When I was informed that my that my seat had been upgraded to first class due to my frequent flyer status, I thought perhaps I had worked myself into a frenzy over nothing. I swung my fifty-plus pound bag into the overhead compartment and took my seat. The flight attendant must've read my mind, because she promptly brought me a glass of water. One more person boarded the flight and took a seat right in front of me. Whew, I wasn't the last one after all.

I chuckled. I felt obligated to explain my tardiness and my sweating and winded state, so I relayed my ordeal in the terminal to the person sitting next to me. The flight crew secured the airplane door and, within minutes, we were airborne. My mind drifted to my business trip, but for some reason, I simply couldn't catch my breath. I usually recover from exercise fairly quickly but I felt so tired and winded, which was unusual to me. I tried to read my book, thinking this might settle me down a bit, and my heart rate did slow a little. I watched the plane take on altitude and, as it did, the cabin pressure began to build. For some reason, I just didn't feel well. Something wasn't right.

Just seven months earlier, my wife and I had decided that I should take an early retirement so we could move to Overland Park, Kansas, to be near our parents and grandchildren. I had been with a major automobile manufacturer for twenty-two years, so before I retired, I had a complete physical check-up with my family physician in Germantown, TN. I also got my teeth cleaned and an eye exam before we made our move. My doctor told me that my blood sugars were a little high and that my cholesterol was a bit elevated but that neither warranted medication. I had my last stress test just two yeas earlier, and the doctor recommended that I get another test sometime in the upcoming year. I didn't think too much about that, since I had no history of heart ailment in my family. My grandfather and my great-grandfather lived into their nineties and were generally in pretty good health. My mother and my father were still living and had no physical complications. I thought I had no reason to worry.

Our plane reached 30,000' and we banked over what I thought was Mankato, MN, and I felt a pressure in my upper body. The pain wasn't immobilizing, but I felt as though someone were sitting on my chest. I felt pain in my right shoulder and arm and fingers were starting to get numb. I felt sweaty, but I didn't feel hot. I had never before experienced the feeling of being clammy. I could feel my heartbeat, but I couldn't catch my breath. I kept wiggling my fingers, trying to get some blood into them. I felt as though there were a lump in my chest. Finally, I ask the flight attendant if she could get an aspirin and a glass of water for me. She had a quizzical look on her face and asked if I was all right. I said I didn't think I was and that I could sure use the aspirin.

I realized what was happening, and I couldn't believe it was happening to me. I had always thought I was in fairly good physical condition. For Pete's sake, I had just moved across country, refurbished a house, started a new traveling job, and had an important business trip to complete. I simply did not have time for this! The pain in my shoulder began to radiate into my arm, and I asked again for that aspirin. The flight attendant asked the passenger next to me to get up. She sat next to me and once again asked if I was okay. I repeated the same negative response as before. She said, "You really don't look well." I mumbled something, but I'm not sure what that something was. She asked me if we needed to do something. I told her that I had pain in my right shoulder symptomatic of a heart attack. "Wouldn't the pain be in your left shoulder if this were a heart attack?" I answered, "No, it is definitely in my right shoulder." My shoulder ached and the pain radiated down my arm and into my hand. Everything felt surreal, and I just couldn't seem to focus. I had a difficult time forming words and remember feeling concerned about any inconvenience to the other passengers.

Suddenly, everything began to go black and my whole body became numb. I could literally feel the life slipping out of me. I knew I was dying—this was the end. As I began to fall into the abyss, I could hear the flight attendant talking to me, but I couldn't understand what she was saying. My last thought was, "God, look after my family, I'm leaving a real mess behind. They just cannot take care of themselves." And that was it. I was gone.

Those who rescued me have told me what happened next.

As I went down, the flight attendant, Nancy Morris, yelled for another flight attendant, Wendy Pickarski. David Collyer, the passenger seated immediately in front of me, stood up and screamed, "I'm an EMT!" Wendy then called out to the passengers, asking if there was a physician on board. Kevin, the passenger just across the aisle from me, jumped up and said, "I'm a trained Emergency Room Nurse!" Without hesitation, they all jumped into action. Nancy quickly went to inform the pilot what was going on. Wendy and the two passengers unbuckled my seat belt and wrestled me to the floor. They checked for a pulse. There was none. I had lost all heart function and brain function. Technically, I was dead. David and Kevin began to apply CPR. They took turns, but the CPR did not revive me. Wendy went in hot pursuit of the AED (Automatic External Defibrillator). They pushed my tie aside and unbuttoned my shirt to expose my chest. They read the brief instructions on the AED and attached the leads to my chest and belly. Wendy and David exchanged a long glance and Wendy said, "Push the button." David pushed the button and a shock surged into my heart.

I immediately came around. A single shock with the defibrillator and my heart restarted.

Medtronic, an AED manufacturer, explains that an AED will monitor your heart rate and blood pressure. If you do not need a shock, it will not deliver one. If the first shock does not bring you back, it will deliver another automatically. There is no danger of being shocked by mistake.

I didn't feel a thing. I just kind of woke up. When I returned to consciousness, my experience was like coming out of a deep well of total blackness as the blood rushed back into my brain. I saw the faces of Wendy and David immediately. My feet were strangely immobile.

I tried to move and to get up. My first thought was that I had fainted. I heard a voice from the direction of my feet and I felt hands shaking there holding my legs in place. Kevin said, "Sir, you have to lie still. You just had a heart attack!" Nancy was standing over him.

There they were, like four angels hovering over me. Now this kid can be pretty smart sometimes, and the concept immediately sunk in. A flood of things hit my brain all at once. One of the first was that I was alive and very much in trouble. I struggled for air. I could not get enough oxygen. They had a portable oxygen tank next to me, and I was gasping for each breath.

Kevin, David, Wendy, and Nancy each asked me questions of one kind or another. In turn, I would ask what my heart rate and my blood pressure were. I was lucid, even if I couldn't breathe. My chest hurt and my lungs burned. They informed me that the pilot, ironically named Peter Paul—a pair of saints, no less—had turned the plane around and was heading back to Minneapolis. Somehow, I made the connection that they might try an emergency landing at one of the local airports. Minneapolis said they could have an emergency team at the plane upon landing.

I was still on the floor, and the ride back to the airport felt like my last ride on the bumper cars at the local amusement park. My chest hurt and I just couldn't breathe. I remember thinking, "If I could just close my eyes and go back to sleep, everything would be all right." I laid there on my back, not knowing if I would survive long enough for the landing. I just knew I'd be okay if only I could just go back to that peaceful place I had been just a short time earlier. David, Wendy, Kevin, and Nancy kept coaching me to stay with them, to not go to sleep. They kept asking me questions, trying to keep me alert. I finally got my aspirin. They kept me alive—and on this side—with their encouragement. They asked questions about my family and told me about theirs. They held my hand, and they stayed right there on the floor with me while we landed. I kept asking about my heart rate and blood pressure as if I understood what they were telling me. Frankly, the numbers didn't make sense–they just seemed high. My heart was racing to try to pump oxygen into my lungs, but my body was not cooperating.

The pilot radioed the Minneapolis airport, and the air traffic controllers cleared the runway for an emergency landing. The pilot came in extremely fast. The moment the plane stopped, the doors flung open and airport security came on board to make sure I was really in a critical state. After he confirmed my condition, Emergency Medical Technicians arrived. They took my vitals, put an oxygen mask on me, attached their monitors to me, and then shifted me onto a hard board and lifted me off the floor.

As I was being taken off the plane, the passengers erupted into cheers and applause! I felt like I had just scored a goal for the "Gipper" in that old Knute Rockney movie. The thought hadn't occurred to me that the passengers were all rooting for me. I could only think of the inconvenience I had caused. I found out much later that one of the passengers was the son of a Sudden Cardiac Arrest Survivor in Minnesota. He called his dad while I was being lifted off and told him that he had found another survivor for his support group. Nancy later told me that everyone was happy and cheerful about the save. She explained that the ground crew then delayed their departure for more than an hour while they searched for a replacement AED and an oxygen bottle.

I held the hands of each of my angels. Each had tears in their eyes. I thanked them and told them that I wanted to know who they were. They each said they would let me know.

The elevator ride down on the outside of the plane was a frigid experience. The day was cold and windy, and light snow swirled in the air. My bare chest was exposed to the elements, and I was still gasping for precious air. Somewhere in the back of my mind, I thought the cold would be good for me, perhaps even slow my heart rate down. I thought about the people who break through ice and their hearts stop yet they come back to life after being warmed. I really wasn't out there that long but my mind was working overtime.

The ambulance had three Emergency Medical Technicians (EMTs), who I fondly think of as "The Three Amigos." These guys were fantastic. They hooked me up to their monitoring equipment, sprayed nitro under my tongue, and asked me a lot of questions. They encouraged me to stay with them. My heart attempted to arrest two more times on the way to the hospital. The EMT's worked with me to keep me lucid and alert. I felt as if my chest were going to explode—I was suffocating and couldn't get enough air in my lungs. The EMT's asked where my billfold was. I actually arched my back, fumbled around, and found my billfold for them thinking that if I died, nothing in there would be very valuable anyway. They wanted to know who I was and who should be contacted. They asked which hospital I wanted to go to. I said I didn't know, as I didn't live there. They suggested Abbott Northwestern in Minneapolis. In the meantime, they provided a constant feed of my vitals to the hospital. They sprayed nitro under my tongue two more times before we arrived at the hospital.

At one point they asked if I was the Patrick Emmett on Findley Way in Apple Valley, MN, or the Patrick Emmett at West 116th Street in Overland Park, KS, or the one in Plano, TX, or the one in Wixom, MI, or the one in Germantown, TN. Who would have known there were so many out there?

I interrupted, "Stop! I'm all of those guys. I moved a lot with my career in the car business."

They laughed and so did I, as best I could.

I said, "That sure is some incredible software you have there. Can you tell me what my tax refund will be next year?"

The information they found covered more than twenty-five years of my medical history. I confirmed my current address with them and they said they had everything they needed. I wasn't sure what that meant, but I was worried about a lengthy check-in procedure at the hospital and how I might settle my fee with the ambulance company. Was this like a cab ride? Did the ambulance need payment that day? I had a lot of questions about what was happening and wondered if I'd even survive to file an insurance claim anyway.

We arrived at the hospital where I was wheeled out of the ambulance and into the emergency room. Now, I've seen a lot of medical shows on TV where the actors go crashing through the doors of the emergency room, and I always thought this was done for dramatic effect. Ha. It's even more spectacular from the perspective of a man who's flat on a gurney! The lights passed over my head, the doors flew open, new faces peered down at me and people talked about me all the time, while I lay there, helpless. All of this swirling activity above me was such a surreal experience.

The time seemed to fly. In only moments, I was in the emergency room with the ER doctor and his staff. Everyone seemed to genuinely care, and they all encouraged me to hang tough. They told me they were going to make me all right. This all sounded good to me, but I had my doubts. By that time, I had decided that I must've had some pretty serious heart problems going on and the best-case scenario was that they were going to crack my chest open and work on my heart. I didn't have high hopes for my survival. Just at this moment in my thought process, my heart attempted to arrest again. My heart went into fibrillation. The heart monitor wasn't exactly music to my ears with its constant "beeeep." I recovered from that round and then a nurse, Linda, smiled at me and told me I was going to make it. She asked for my wife's phone number.

"I, uh, I don't know what the number is, but my cell phone is in my pocket."

I was entangled in wires, hose, and life support, but I managed to fish the cell phone out of my pocket and hand the thing to her. I told her to open the phone and go to "contacts," find Marilyn, and then hit send. She called my wife. I didn't know how Linda would accomplish that phone call without causing a complete panic at home, but she did. She was outstanding.

Marilyn and I have been married for thirty-four years. We are corporate campaigners. We've moved fourteen times in the years we've been together. We've been through a lot—but nothing like this. I knew the news would be difficult for Marilyn to hear. She had been shopping at a *Hobby Lobby* by herself that morning and answered her cell phone in the store. Linda introduced herself to Marilyn over the phone and explained that I had experienced a heart attack. Linda told her that I was in the emergency room and was hanging in there. She told Marilyn not to rush to Minnesota just yet—Linda told her to wait for word from the hospital and then told Marilyn that she'd be in touch as things progressed. Their conversation was calm and settling. Linda held the phone to my ear so I could tell Marilyn that, while I wasn't ready to run a marathon, I was getting the best possible care.

Linda had an odd look on her face. I knew she had something to say.

"We have to get you out of these things. You know that time that your mother kept telling you about? You know…the one when you might need clean underwear? Well, this is that time."

As she helped me out of my clothes, I was trying to think of some bawdy comeback, but, this time, I was too embarrassed to reply. She held my hand and smiled.

"Don't worry; I'll be with you the whole way."

There were three doctors in the emergency room and a large support staff. They performed an "Echo scan" on my heart, which is similar to the equipment used for a pregnant woman so that doctors—and the mom—might view her unborn child. They conferred, made introductions, and I nodded agreeably as if I understood who everyone was and what they were telling me.

I waited for the news that I would have to undergo heart bypass surgery. One of the doctors explained that I had complete blockage of the main coronary artery that goes into the heart. He said that I couldn't get any oxygen from my lungs to my heart as a result of the blockage. That's why I had so much trouble breathing. They proposed a couple of options, but the only terms I heard were "angioplasty" and "un-invasive." The doctor also explained the stent procedure—and what the consequences of placement meant to not insert the stent. He, of course explained that there is risk. He wanted me to understand that I would have to make that decision at this time very quickly. As he was talking, his words turned to "blah, blah, blah," and I just blurted out, "I've already died; what's one more risk? Let's do it!"

By this time, the whole process had become a team sport. I had an entourage just like the hip hop guys. We took the elevator up to another floor, and I tried wisecracking with the nurse, Linda. She wasn't buying any of it. I even tried arresting again. Some people will do anything to get all of the attention. We went into the operating theater. I kept looking around to see if anyone was eating popcorn, but I only saw white coats.

Drs. Peterson, Wang, and Lawler attended to me in the Catheter Laboratory Operating Theatre. Linda stayed with me the whole way, as she said she would. I found all of this very interesting for sure, and I was awake during the whole procedure. I tried to remain detached and maintain an academic interest in what they were doing, but on some level, I really didn't want to know. They made a small incision and slipped the catheter into an artery in my groin. They were glued to this TV screen as if they were watching the NBA playoffs. Meanwhile, I felt disappointed about being left out of the fun. I wanted to be up there with them. I heard Dr. Wang explain that they had cleared the blockage. They said I looked much better, but I didn't seem to feel better, not right away. I was still trying to breathe. They told me I would begin to feel better shortly, but that I shouldn't move. I did my best to obey orders, because I really didn't want to go through anything worse. I heard the announcement that the stent had been placed and they were withdrawing the catheter from the artery.

I laid there cold, weak, and flaccid, gasping for breath, trying to be still, convincing myself not to be embarrassed about my nakedness. Several things swirled through my mind–the death experience and what had happened to me up to that point was at the top of the list. I thought about being naked before my maker and that such things really didn't matter. I thought about where I had been and tried to sort through all of my feelings. Then all at once, I really did begin to breathe more easily. I was told I looked pink. I was grateful that I had nothing on that would clash with pink. I tried to ask a question and was told to lie still and everything would be fine. The doc closed the artery and provided me with a serious admonition–if I moved over the next twenty-four hours, I could bleed to death. I realized that laying flat on my back for twenty-four hours would get mighty uncomfortable. The doctors congratulated me, and I was wheeled out of the theater and into the Cardio Intensive Care unit.

Ah, I thought I could finally get some rest. But alas, I became a popular person. My fifteen minutes of fame at Abbott Northwestern had just begun. Word spread of my emergency landing at the airport, my rush to the hospital and the stent placement—all successful. I no sooner was placed in my bed than I had hospital guests. A fireball nurse, Barbara, came into my room. She was glowing. She declared that I had just experienced the "Level One Rapid Response" program. She proudly announced that from the time the airplane doors were opened until the stent placement procedure was complete; the total elapsed time was forty-three minutes. I had become a poster child for everything going right. This was my lucky day after all. Doctors from all over the hospital came to visit. Dr. Lawler came in and showed me a picture of my heart with the main coronary artery all marked out in black. That's where the blockage was. I had 100% blockage, which was why I couldn't get any oxygen into my heart.

Everyone was happy! I have to admit it—I felt pretty good, too. We called my wife, and we called my mother, who was eighty years old. She took the news pretty well–I was surprised. The hospital took on a kind of party atmosphere. The doctors, nurses, EMT's, they were all rooting for me. All I wanted to do at this point was sleep—the healthy kind of sleep.

Later, I woke up and felt groggy. I had been sedated, and I had an even bigger problem. I woke up in the late evening. I had a new nurse, and told her that I had to pee. She thought she was being helpful when she came in and warned me not to move because "I would bleed to death." That's pretty good motivation not to move, for sure but I had been lying in the same position for more than nine hours with a sandbag on my crotch. This was to hold everything in place so I didn't open the artery and, as was so gently put, bleed to death. I understood all of this, but nature called, and I was on my back, trying my best to hold my own.

Finally, the nurse came in with what looked like a wine carafe (could have been in its former life) and she seemed pleased that she held the solution. But this was no easy feat–I was lying hori-zontally with a vertical body part, trying to hit a horizontal object, so the laws of physics went right out the window. I made a mighty attempt. Since I was on my own, I cheated and leaned a little onto my left to try to hit the mark. I quit, laid back, and tried to think of things in the desert.

I went back to sleep after the nurse left the room, and then about a couple of hours later, I was awake again. I knew I didn't want the same woman to help me any more. I rang the bell and Jason, a Cardio Intensive Care nurse, walked through the door. Yes! The shifts had changed. I told him I had to pee and that I had been in misery for some time. He looked at me, and he looked at the bottle.

"Hey, man, you can't do that. Let me help you."

He did, too. He helped me keep my sandbag in place, and we swung off the edge of the bed onto the floor, he pulled the curtain around me where I stood and enjoyed the most gratifying elimination in my lifetime. Sometimes, you just really don't know what you are grateful for in this life, until you are presented with them.

The next day, I was up and walking around. Barbara came back in and told me that word had gotten out that about the re-markable chain of events surrounding my survival. She asked if it was okay for Fox News to come in and interview me for the evening news. I said that I had no objection, that I welcomed the opportunity to thank everyone who was involved. Throughout the day, I had several doctors and nurses stop by to visit. David and Kevin, Nancy and Wendy all called that day to see how I was. I gave them my e-mail address and told them I wanted to hear from them.

My employer called, as did other friends who had heard of my ordeal. My wife, Marilyn, arrived around noon and was a welcome sight. I felt pretty good about everyone wishing me well.

The nursing staff was fantastic. I moved from intensive care to a room on the cardio recovery ward. They were all very attentive and willing to educate me about what had happened and what I needed to be doing from this time forward. I discovered that my blood sugars had shot through the roof, and that my cholesterol was very high, and my blood pressure was a bit elevated too. Everything was topsy-turvy.

The nurses began to introduce me to some of the many medications I would need to take for a while. They started me on Lovenox to prevent blood clots. Lovenox is a liquid injected into the belly. I asked if Lovenox was like Viagra. They said no and wondered why I asked.

"Well, you know, 'Love Knocks'?"

I was disappointed, but what can you do. They put me on Cumadon for the same reason. I was provided a dose of Plavix too. This medication was described as a kind of "Slick 50" or "Teflon" for the blood, to prevent further plaque build-up in the arteries, especially in my newly placed stent. I asked if Plavix was extracted from the duck-billed Plavix from southern Australia. They really didn't know what I was talking about. I was put on Lipitor for cholesterol, Actos for my sugar, and a blood pressure medicine, as well as aspirin and a bottle of nitroglycerin. When I left that hospital, I was a walking pharmacy. I could put Barry Bonds to shame. By the time I left the hospital, I could single-handedly support half of the TV programs I watch in the evenings.

I was in the hospital for a total of three days. Nancy and Wendy came by and brought a pot of tulips. They were terrific. Nancy then came back and drove Marilyn and me to the Minneapolis airport—she also helped me get through security. I was so grateful to Northwest Airlines for having AEDs on board and for saving my life that I thanked everyone I met. They were clueless as to what I was talking about, but they seemed satisfied that a customer was being nice to them. I sympathized with their bankruptcy and wished them a speedy recovery. I am still grateful to the men and women of Northwest Airlines for their foresight in having emergency medical equipment and trained personnel on hand for situations like mine. My gratitude goes out to a great many people. In total, there had to have been more than a hundred people, in one way or another, involved in my rescue that blustery day in January. Together, they had launched me back to life, giving me a second chance. I know I had a lot of people rowing my boat ashore. Thanks to each and every one of you.

2

The After-Death Experience

The subject of death is never an easy one to face. Since so many people have asked about what happened when I was unconscious, I feel that I should share my death experience.

Everyone wants to know the same thing. "Did you see the 'bright light'?" "What was death like?"

The mind is an incredible organ and is capable of far more than we can begin to understand. My impression of what happened after I collapsed and died are what I recall, the way I remember the things that happened to me—that is what I will share with you.

I am not about to debate the metaphysical issues of personal or religious beliefs with anyone. After hearing my story, one woman approached me with the notion that death is final and that there is nothing after we die. She wanted to debate the point. I didn't rise to the bait. I won't change any one person's mind on what they choose to believe.

My Sudden Cardiac Death experience left me on the floor of that airplane with no brain function or heart function for nearly five minutes. That's pretty final. All I can do is relate my experience, as I believe them to have occurred. You do not have to believe me, you will find out for yourself soon enough what there is beyond this life experience. Life can be pretty short, after all.

Our expectations of death are based on fear, myth, religious perceptions, and hope. We are taught and trained from birth to accept certain beliefs and feelings concerning the subject. In my sociology classes at the university, we would refer to these beliefs as folkways and mores. We discovered for most people, it's basic human nature to want to fit in with what others believe. No one wants to be singled out as being different and excluded from the group. You are probably reading this right now with a great deal of skepticism. I hope you are, because only through skepticism and questioning can we expand our knowledge of things we do not know or understand.

My own death experience began while I was talking to the flight attendant on the airplane. I had dull pain in my chest and right shoulder and my arm and hand were becoming numb. I became dizzy and as I began to loose consciousness I had an overwhelming sense of dying. I said a prayer to myself for God to look after my family because I was leaving a mess behind.

I am the breadwinner of several family members. Many people rely on me. Sometimes I feel like I am the only guy rowing in a canoe full of people. I had one daughter left in college and living at home. Her boyfriend of six years had moved from another part of the country and was living in a spare bedroom. My twentyfour-year-old son, recently divorced, had lost his job and just moved back into the lower level of our house. His two-year-old son was now living with us four days a week. My oldest daughter began a job as a department head of an English department in a local college and was asking us for help by watching her one-and-a-half year-old daughter from time to time. Between my aging parents and my wife's aging mother we felt like we had our hands full. I had just begun working as an automotive consultant after years of working for a major automobile manufacturer. As I collapsed, I knew I was dying and would leave all of these unanswered concerns behind. To my mind, I was leaving a mess.

Right after the Automatic External Defibrillator (AED) delivered the electric shock into my body, I felt like I was coming up out of a dark deep well. All I remember of that experience was black. Slowly, the black began to dissipate, and I felt a tingling sensation through out my body as I slowly came into consciousness. The faces above me came into focus and I saw my four rescuers—whom I consider my four angels—above me. My feet seemed oddly immobilized, and I suddenly became aware that I was lying on the floor with David at my head and Kevin holding my feet. I had that ozone taste in my mouth, and I was embarrassed because I thought that I had fainted. I apologized and tried to get up. I was immediately told to lie still because I had just suffered a heart attack. I heard them but thought that surely they must be wrong. Then it hit me—I could not breathe, I was struggling for each gasp of air. My chest felt a major constriction and

I experienced some pain, but that was not what was occupying my mind.

My rescuers asked if I could talk, and I was lucid enough to give my name between breaths. They explained that they had delivered a shock to me with an AED and that I must lie still until they could get the plane on the ground. The reality hadn't yet sank in. I had had a heart attack and these kind people were attending to me. My mind began to buzz, thinking about many things. Being a consummate traveler, I expressed my concern about the other passengers on the plane and the delay in their travel plans. I was told to not worry about them and to concentrate on staying with the living.

Frequently, I would ask questions about my heart rate and blood pressure. They were telling me the numbers but, honestly, none of this really made sense to me. My heart rate was well above 104, which seemed high. In fact, my heart rate could have been much higher. I don't know. I was just trying to demonstrate that I was still with them and could communicate.

My wonderful rescuers kept encouraging me to hang in there and not to fall into slumber. On the floor of the airplane, holding the hands of my earthly angels, I was on the verge of repeated arresting from lack of oxygen and without normal heart function. I desperately fought the urge to give in.

At the time, death really didn't seem like such a bad option to me. The experience was serene and sustaining. Death was inviting, and I felt compelled to go back. I knew, of course, that I couldn't, so I hung on. Those who monitored my heart rhythm told me that I nearly arrested four more times on my way to the hospital and twice more in the emergency room. My heart was in fibrillation. Instead of a normal heart beat, my heart quivered and could not eject blood with any kind of rhythm.

While I was lying on the floor of the airplane, gasping for breath, moments after my revival, a flood of images and feelings swept into my brain. I thought about where I had been and what I had been doing prior to being resuscitated. The first impression I got was that wherever I had been, seemed very good to me. I was comfortable there and I didn't want to leave. I've never had a death wish, but it just seemed so simple. It would have been easy to just close my eyes, fall asleep, and go back to where it was so peaceful. I remember light and being surrounded by many souls. I definitely felt that I was in the presence of God.

The second thing that immediately came to mind was that you leave all your earthly beliefs and feelings behind. I think I knew what that meant at the time. The feeling was you leave all of your manmade inventions and accumulations with your body when you pass to the other side. This includes your politics, religion, race, and feelings about things you do here on earth. All those things are shed like a coat when you move through that portal. I also thought there were some emotions that you do take with you—like love and loyalty and a sense of family. I felt a closeness and a connection with the souls that surrounded me while I was at this place.

These things just started drifting into my mind along with images of where I had just been. I cannot tell you where I had been but this place seemed to have a lot of light. I was a comfortable there and I was welcome. Everything there seemed vast and full of wonder. I felt no pain and knew that I was not in my physical human form and these things did not seem to matter. I was there for what must have been a very long time. I met many people I knew, some of them family members, and had many conversations. I do not remember anyone being in their earthly human form but they were all familiar, just the same.

Yes, the thing that quickly impressed me was that there was definitely a God. I got the sense that God was not a single being. God was neither a man nor a woman, but more like a collection of souls. The image that comes to mind is being in the presence of great intellectual intensity. Remembering this impression and trying to remember what the souls looked like is like looking at a hazy photograph. These impressions are hard to define because I also had the feeling that I was told a great many things and that I was not supposed to remember everything that happened to me, not just yet. What seemed to me like shapeless, out of focus images may just be my mind's attempt at interpreting things that I can not relate to in this physical world.

When I tell my story, this part often frustrates many people. They want me to tell them things that reinforce their particular beliefs. I have religious convictions that have not changed as a result of my experience with death. In fact, they reinforce my faith. I will not make up stories to satisfy someone's notion of what God or heaven or hell should be like. Just trust that there is a God and there is a place to go when you die.

As I stood before this all—knowing presence, I had the distinct impression that I had discussed a great many things. My life was reviewed and God explained to me that, in a sense, my life was "perfect"—the way things were intended to be. Perhaps I felt as though it was perfect because there was an order to things, and all of life's events fell into place. I got the impression that there was a future that had yet to take place and that I was meant to be a part of it. I was told I needed to return to complete this part of the future. I was also told that I wouldn't remember everything that happened while I was there, but everything would reveal itself in due course, that "events would unfold." I sensed that I must be patient and return to live a good life…a longer life. Mine wasn't over.

I know that I had asked a lot of questions, and that I received many answers about things in my life and living on earth. I know we spoke of the meaning of life, the nature of how things work, answers about the universe, and of course, we discussed religion. The most important thing I remember learning was that we are all here to serve on earth for a short time before we return to eternity. When I was asked later by friends how I would know what to remember and what not to remember, one answer resounded from deep within me, "You have to trust yourself. You will know–we all do, down deep inside, all of the things we need to know, what we are here for and what we need to do while we are here."

Religion was on my mind that day and my impression of my conversation with God was that religion and spirituality is an important part of life on earth. I also got the impression that much of what we practice of religion on earth is man made in nature and it is one of the things you leave behind when you pass to the other side. Whether you are Christian, Jewish, Muslim, or pagan, it's all the same on the other side. Religion and spirituality is an important part of humanity on earth as a divinely inspired tool used to comfort one another and provide answers to the great questions that elude understanding. Religious beliefs are meant to guide us while we are here on earth—a blueprint for our behavior and a compass to give us direction. Our mission isn't to dispute religion with each other or debate theology–life is primarily about living good and healthy lives and assisting others in this effort as well. It seems to me that a lot of people are really focused on each others differences. They feel more comfortable with their culture or set of beliefs. Rather than look for the things that can draw people together, the things we have in common, they want to set themselves apart. While I was on the other side, I got the feeling that this was not really acceptable behavior.

Working on doing the right thing, helping others, and respecting the things we share in common with other people are things that I have heard all of my life. This all seemed like pretty simple stuff, yet how often do we practice this way of life?

I remember a great deal but I do not remember everything. I don't remember any discussions that I may have had about murderers, thieves, and people who take advantage and abuse others in this world. If I was told anything about the fate of these people, it did not come back with me. There must be some answers yet to discover. My only impression was that once we passed through to the other side, we are all pure souls and all pretty much the same. I didn't get an impression of any kind of elitist system or ranking of souls based on goodness or sins committed or even piety while we are here on earth. The notion of judgment may be there but it was not a part of my experience.

I received the impression from God that we are all spirits invested into the earthly bodies of animals, subject to the many chemical imbalances that can occur in that form. We must do the best we can and enjoy the physical experience of life on earth while we can. When we leave this earth, we move into another level of existence. Just that!

You must understand that these are my impressions of what happened to me. I have had the unique opportunity to meet many other Sudden Cardiac Arrest survivors. The one thing that bonds all of us together is that each of us had died.

Not everyone who has died experiences the same thing. I did not, for example, have the out-of-body experience of floating above myself on the floor of the airplane. Perhaps that was because I was already in the air on that airplane. I saw no brilliant flashes of light and, to my recollection, I didn't meet any family members. Other survivors that I have spoken to did have some of these experiences, and they are as real to them as my experiences are to me. There is no conflict. Any and all of these things can happen when you pass on.

About one third of the survivors that I speak to, have no memory of the death experience. In fact, they have no memory of their cardio event at all. This is not uncommon. The brain will block out what may be perceived as an unpleasant experience. The single common thread for all of us who have passed on is that there is definitely another place to go. We will go there, all of us, when our time comes.

The day that I died I was sent back, not rejected, but sent back to complete some earthly mission. I carry with me the notion that "events will unfold." I wasn't meant to remember everything about the other side, and I wasn't supposed to know the exact reason for returning. This was what I found so frustrating with my recovery effort for several months after my event. I wanted to know what it I am supposed to do, so I can get this thing done and over with. You really have to love a task-oriented person.

Other Sudden Cardiac Arrest survivors that I have spoken to remember coming back and talking with loved ones before resuscitation. Others talk of taking an incredible journey and some speak of seeing the face of Jesus or a special saint before coming back to earth. The essence of floating above their lifeless bodies is common. One woman remembers going into a separate room and discussing her condition with someone, then returning and getting back into her body before being revived. There are stories of brilliant lights, beautiful gardens, and conversations with relatives and friends. Vibrant colors, personal conversations with living family members, even negotiations with a supernatural force or spirit to return to life are shared in various accounts. These experiences are all true and very real to every survivor.

The one thing that almost all survivors experience is the simple fact that there is absolutely nothing to fear when your time comes. No one I spoke to had any impression of hellfire, damnation, or angels sitting on clouds plucking on harps. The common experience was everything seemed quite natural and comforting.

Everyone who has died will tell you that being sent back was a miracle. Science may have been involved, but there was an agreement on the other side for their return. People from every culture and every walk of life have experienced death and returned to tell what has happened to them. The thing that may seem in conflict is that the stories are different. I believe that the death experience is unique to each of us. We all go to the other side and there may be variations on how we interpret what we see and experience when we return. I don't think we exist in that other place in our earthly forms and I don't think we communicate as we do on earth but I do believe that when we return, our brains translate what happened into a way we can understand. That is why the stories are so different. Our brains must rely on prior knowledge and experience to make sense of the encounter.

Most of the survivors I have spoken to, however, talk only of the survival experience. Conversations concerning the death experience are not forthcoming. I don't pry, but if the survivor chooses to talk about his or her experience, I will listen. I continue to meet and discuss this very sensitive issue with survivors. This is a very personal and sensitive area for most people who have had the death experience and when they agree, I share their stories because through them there is hope for more people to survive Sudden Cardiac Death.

One survivor told me of his death experience that actually saved his life. He had been out mowing his lawn on a hot summer day. He became dizzy and collapsed on his front yard. Across town his daughter was washing the dishes. Her three-year-old son was at the kitchen table having breakfast and he began a conversation with someone. With her back turned she asked him who he was talking to. The little boy said "Grandpa, and he told me be to be a good boy and that I was going to grow up and be a businessman and have a family. He said that he will miss me but I will be OK." The daughter dropped her kitchen towel, turned around and looked at her son. Immediately, she reached for the phone and called her mother and asked "Where's Dad?" Her mother responded by looking out her front room window and saw him lying on the ground. She hung up and immediately dialed 911. The local police department had just received AED's in their vehicles the prior week and a squad car was only one block from the house. When they arrived, the first responders applied several shocks to revive the man who had collapsed in his yard. He arrested twice on the way to the hospital and again in the Emergency room. He made it! He survived because of a conversation he had with his grandson during his death experience.

The death experience is something that only happens once to most people in a lifetime. A few—very few—have had the opportunity to slip through a portal in the space-time continuum into another dimension and return again. All of us who have been there are physically and emotionally altered forever for the experience.

I do know this–I will try to take the best possible care of what is left of my physical body while I can with the time I have left. I know that I am damaged and will never be the same. But I will perform the best I can as a fellow human being to love and respect others. Once we pass on to the other side, we will all be the same–there will be no rich, no poor, no powerful, no weak, no pious, no heretic, no skin color, no anger, and no judgment…just the promise of eternal beauty and peace.

I encourage anyone who is reading this book to make the most of your life experience, to respect others and to be good stewards of this fragile earth. Enjoy life, seek happiness in others, and carry these sensations to the other side with you. Remember, everything you own is someone else's stuff when you pass on. So don't hold on to your possessions too tightly. Hold on to your joys, for those are what you'll take with you.

3

Coping With Survival

For the longest time after my Sudden Cardiac Arrest, I struggled with the significance of my survival. The simple odds of survival are remarkably narrow. According to the Sudden Cardiac Arrest Foundation, "The average survival rate from a Sudden Cardiac Arrest is 6% to 7% (Pre-hospital Emergency Care 1997; 1(1): 45-57). Knowing this, I've had many one-sided discussions with God asking why I was sent back and what really is my purpose? I have had some pretty tough dialogue, albeit one sided.

The hospital did a fantastic job of taking care of me while I was there. I was in Intensive Care for twenty four hours, and then placed into a cardio unit for observation and testing. I was poked, probed, x-rayed, surveyed and counseled.

Within the first eighteen hours, the hospital was so delighted with the Rapid Response that they asked if I was okay having the local Fox News station to come up and interview me in my intensive care room. By this time I had already been out of my bed and on my feet a couple of times. I knew that I was happy to be alive and breathing but I really had no idea what an incredible effort everyone contributed to get me to this point. The camera crew came in, I was interviewed in my bed and I made the evening news. I had my fifteen minutes of fame.

The complete gravity of what had happened to me had not yet hit home. I knew I had experienced a heart attack and was told by hospital staff that I would have to do things in a very different way. They had me up on my feet and moving around with in a day or so of admission. I felt safe around all of the competent people who seemed very interested in my well being. In fact, I had a sense of loss and a little trepidation as I left the hospital and returned to my home and the struggles that lay ahead for me.

People simply do not return to the routine of their lives after a heart attack or a sudden cardiac arrest. New challenges arise each day. Just dealing with the fact that I survived death was a source of conflict in my mind. I found that surviving simply wasn't enough. I had to cope with all of the new changes to my body and physical regimen. I had medications that wrecked havoc with how I felt from day to day. I had to overcome depression and deal with why I was spared and asked to return to life. I began to think of my daily routine as coping with survival.

Marilyn and I flew home and during my in-home recovery, I was careful about virtually everything. My Sudden Cardiac Arrest event scared the life out of me. I knew that with one wrong step, I would be back in the hospital or worse, dead again. Knowing that I was sent back for a reason, death was not an option.

Marilyn and I put together meal plans I had to find a local family physician and a cardiologist. We had not lived in this part of the country more than a few months following my early retirement. I had not made any medical arrangements. Now was the time to do that.

I found a great family physician through my health care provider. He recommended several cardiologists in the area. I found one, made an appointment and went through the process of telling them what happened. I began taking blood tests, stress tests, EKG's and consultation. I followed up almost weekly with my family physician at his request.

One of the drugs that was prescribed to me to thin my blood during this time was Warfarin. In an effort to get the proper dosage, I needed to have my blood tested weekly and then report the findings to both my family physician and the cardiologist. This became more of a grind than a routine. At one point, there was a mixed message between what the cardiologist and the family physician were recommending.

In the weeks following my cardiac arrest, my body was still trying to heal itself. I felt that exercise was critical so I would often take walks in the mornings with my dog, Faye. She is a German shepherd with tremendous insight. She is my daughter's dog, yet she knew that I wasn't well and began sleeping near the foot of my bed at night. She just kind of adopted me as her pet. Faye's nattering in the morning forces me to take that two- to four-mile walk, even if I don't want to. My conversations with God seemed to have had absolutely no effect on her. I'm sure she thought I was talking to the squirrels along the wooded path we walk.

Recovery during the weeks and months that followed my release from the hospital was much slower I wanted. My dog Faye was the only one I could talk with. She and I would walk up and down the streets and the trails around my neighborhood. During my recovery that winter, I felt cold and lonely on my daily walks, even with my dog. I also harbored resentment that I was sent back for reasons that were unclear to me, and I saw little purpose or meaning in my daily life at the time. The recovery process was a slow struggle.

My family was subjected to my short temper, and they lovingly bore with me. I demonstrated little patience with rude people, with people who ran stop signs, with selfishness in others, people's political views, world events as I saw them, and pretty much everyone in my world in general, as self-serving and foolish. Most people have a degree of feelings about these things, but I was pretty damn angry. The extreme mood swings were icing on the cake. I had become a different person from the person I was before my event.

With in three to four weeks, I returned to traveling with my job. I was back in airports and meeting rigorous business schedules. I felt that I needed to return to work both to earn money and to keep my mind off of the things that were bothering me. I just got worse. I probably went back to this lifestyle too fast. I should have allowed myself more recovery time.

I didn't find out until much later that most of my mood swings were a result of my body trying to heal itself, and my body chemistry struggling to make adjustment to the many medications introduced to my system.

I had also become something of a food nazi. I had literally cut everything out of my diet that I felt certain might kill me. At the time, I was struggling with being a diabetic and how that affected my body. My cholesterol numbers were very high and I was in a race to get them under control. My diet and eating habits had a very negative effect on my outlook. Mostly, however, I resented being returned to this life with these problems, and I was hesitant to ask questions from doctors and other people in my life, because no one seemed to have the answers. I felt as though I had no one to share these feelings with and I didn't even want to admit them to myself. I felt depressed and helpless. I felt pathetic.

I started cardio rehab at the hospital a couple of months after my return home. At the time I did not feel a real bond with the other patients in the program. I was traveling frequently with my job, so I was not in the rehab program as regularly as someone who was visiting the center every day because of a heart attack. Also, I was walking every day, sometimes up to four miles a day. I was driven and determined to single-handedly overcome my physical disability.

Because of my irregular visits to the rehab center, some of the staff seemed to worry that I wasn't getting much out of the program. I felt independent, not needing a coach, and they sensed that attitude in me. They really did their best with me—I was simply not as responsive to their program as they had wished. Cardio rehab is good, however there did not seem to be anyone who could relate to my sudden cardiac arrest event. Most of these patients had heart problems that they had been living with for some time. Mine just crept up on me and slapped me in the face.

I have since spoken to other Sudden Cardiac Arrest patients and many of them agreed that they too felt different than the heart patients in the Cardio Rehab program at first but in the long run, all heart patients have much in common. A cardio rehab program is critical in helping that patient come to grips with their condition and how to manage their health. I was just too stubborn at the time to listen.

I actually lost the use of some of my heart. At the time I was exercising in cardio rehab, I really did not know how much of my heart had been damaged and permanently lost. While the exercise from cardio rehab was good, it was only part of what I needed for recovery. My doctors had prescribed a medical treatment to flood the heart with as much oxygen rich blood as possible in an attempt to help the heart muscle recover damaged tissue. Still, at this stage, just four months after my event, with the many changes in my medications and just my general health, I didn't feel better. I felt worse.

Of course, I was worse. I had literally lost a piece of my heart, like in the song by Janis Joplin. The cardiologist finally told me that my Ejection Fraction was between 24% and 30%. There was some confusion in the test results, and I kept taking stress tests to get to a good result. The bottom line was that I had permanent damage to 10% to 12% of my heart. My heart would never recover, and I would not be the same as I was before the event. From that day forward, my heart had to work harder with what was left.

Unfortunately, my lifestyle at the time didn't give me the break I needed to heal. I was traveling for my job, flying to locations all over the country to work as an automotive consultant. I could end up in a different state every week. Sometimes I would travel two or three weeks in a row, and then I would be home for a week or two. My schedule was fairly inconsistent, and this certainly wasn't the best therapy for a person recovering from heart problems. I probably started traveling too quickly after my SCA event. I really needed some down time, and I was still changing medications frequently. Some of them were having an incredible effect on my body and brain. One of the medicines had my blood pressure so low that I was fainting. The cholesterol drugs affected my liver function. My blood sugars were bouncing all over the place like the commodities market after a hurricane. My physical condition was weak and erratic. My moods were up and down and most of the time I simply felt lost and alone.

I was five months into my recovery and now felt like I needed a change. I needed to take stock. I then remembered some training I had received as a Boy Scout leader many years ago. We moved a lot with my job during those years, as my son was going through scouts. We kept up with scouting programs in four different states. As a youth, I became an Eagle Scout and my son became one as well. It was a quite an experience for both of us. The scouting experiences my son and I shared were some of the closest we had ever been as father and son. Through many camping adventures and leadership programs we learned to understand our environment.

One of the many life experiences taught to us in the scouting program was survival. For example, what would you do if you suddenly found yourself lost in a wilderness, disoriented, and perhaps even injured? How would you react? Would you panic? People who have gone through a life-changing event such as a Sudden Cardiac Arrest are often faced with similar challenges. Survival is a learned skill that takes using everything you have to understand the world around you and how to adapt.

One day, while I was cleaning up some old boxes that we had stored, I stumbled across an old book that we used years ago to instill some basic values in the boys in our scout troop. What I found was the US Army Field Manual 21-76 on survival. I thumbed through the pages and couldn't believe my eyes as I read from the pages. Everything I needed to do was right there on the pages in front of me. The book hit right to the heart of what I needed to do.

The US Army Field Manual 21-76 sums up survival as follows: "*It takes much more than the knowledge and skills to build shelters, get food, make fires, and travel without the aid of standard navigational devices to live successfully through a survival situation. Some people with little or no survival training have managed to survive life-threatening circumstances. Some people with survival training have not used their skills and died. A key ingredient in any survival situation is the mental attitude of the individual(s) involved. Having survival skills is important; having the will to survive is essential. Without a desire to survive, acquired skills serve little purpose and invaluable knowledge.*" Those are pretty powerful words, and they apply to self-healing, too.

With the advent of reality TV, many people might first think of a TV show when the term "survivor" is mentioned. Those same people might also think about how a survivor needs to last several weeks on a TV program. There's some truth to that. The contestants on those programs are subjected to events and a test of their ability to conquer fear and failure. Surviving a heart attack or a Sudden Cardiac Arrest is really no different.

I began to make a list of everything I remembered. As a boy scout, if I got lost, I would stop what I was doing, assess my surroundings, and try to focus–in short, I would make a list. Then I would try to get a fix on the time of day, how far I might be from other people, and think about what other options I may have. If I felt that I was truly lost, and I couldn't walk out, I would try to make an emergency camp and focus on what I was going to do until help could find me.

My next step would be to determine my personal physical condition to see if I had any injuries that needed attention. I would then take an inventory of my resources by emptying my pockets, my backpack, or anything else I had. I'd lay everything out on the ground in front of me and take stock of what I had and how I could adapt what I had for survival. For example, I would look for anything I could use as a signaling device or something that would start a fire.

I remembered that the most important thing I would need is water. It's possible to live without food for a few days but certainly not without water. If I did not have potable drinking water, I'd have to find some. Then I would consider my food options, if any were available to me. And I'd need to seek shelter quickly. I knew I'd have to pick one that would be out of the wind and would protect me from the rain and cold.

As I made my list, I thought about fire. Fire was important because it not only provided warmth, but boiled water would kill parasites, and would help to cook raw meat to make it edible. Finally, I'd have to engineer a plan of action for both short-term and long-term survival.

I actually did spend two nights on my own in a survival mode with little or no gear while I was a boy in scouting. It was a good experience. I sure made a lot of hungry biting insects happy those two nights.

It didn't occur to me at first that my heart condition and subsequent cardiac arrest were, indeed, a survival situation. As I made my list I came to the conclusion that I would have to make some changes, or I wouldn't survive.

My first instinct was to take an inventory of my assets. When I get confused and can't figure things out in my life, I always make lists. Sorting things out and prioritizing them has always seemed to help me make sense of things. I began to write down what I had in my life and list those things that felt I needed to survive.

I began with those things that were basic and the closest to me—I had my life. I had survived a Sudden Cardiac Arrest, and I was alive and walking around. Number two was that I actually possessed purpose, as does everyone else on this planet. My list grew—I have a wonderful wife who has been devoted to me for thirty-four years. That would make her a better survivor than me. She is my rock and my best friend. We've been through thick and thin together. That makes Marilyn a pretty good asset.

My list went on…I have three children who are young adults and also making their imprint on this world. I rely on each of them as much in some ways as they rely on me in others. They are the bread and butter of my soul. I have a personal, unique, and different relationship with each one of them. I believe in them, and I'd like to believe that they think of me as a spiritual guide for them as well.

As my list went on, I considered our two grandchildren who were the focus of a great deal of attention for my wife and me. These little ones looked to my wife and me as special people in their lives, and I looked to them as a boundless source of pure love. Somehow, I felt that my mission on earth—the reason I returned—was in someway connected to them.

I listed that I am also very fortunate to still have my parents with me. They are very lucid, and they practice the art of uncon-ditional love, which has sustained me most of my life. Also on the list was that I was fortunate to have a job and work for some very nice and understanding people. It became clear that travel right after my event was the source of some of my stress. I also felt that I could do better at my work, if only I felt better. I listed other things that are in my support system like my church, my dog, and friends that I have made over the years. I had family, but I also felt that I needed to improve the relationship between this support system and myself. Okay, metaphorically speaking, I had shelter. What else did I need?

I assessed my physical condition. I felt as though I was making progress but I also knew I needed to adjust my sails. I looked at my exercise program, my diet, and my medications. These were areas that all needed some help.

I knew needed to improve my diet, so I made arrangements to visit a dietician. I needed a greater selection of food and more balance in my diet. The lady I went to was just the ticket. I began to eat better, and the result? I began to feel better! With food off my list, I paged down my list.

The next step was a dramatic one—I changed cardiologists. Each person must make a judgment about his or her own situation, but the one I had just wasn't working out for me. The combination of drug therapy wasn't working and I had too many confusing test results. Too often I felt as though there was a lack of interest in my condition. I needed to make a change. Most doctors agree that you have to have confidence in your doctor in order to make any headway in your physical condition. It doesn't hurt to shop around.

Water is another basic of survival. I began to drink more water and become more hydrated. I now carry water with me when I work, and I drink water frequently throughout the day.

Fire is more of a metaphor for how you perceive life—and I needed some motivation in my life. My motivation was driven in part by how I felt as a result of my medication therapy. I was determined to get my blood sugars within a normal range, and I wanted my cholesterol under control too. That is why I ate the way I did. I began to eat fish once or twice a week instead of three or four times a week. I didn't grow up eating fish and, while I know its healthy food, I just don't like fish that much. To help me in this effort, I began to take 1,000 mg of Omega[3] fish oil three times a day. You need to understand that these are things that I have done for myself. I am not a doctor and in no way am I offering, you as a reader, any medical advice. I have sought professional care and rely on their advice and I suggest you do the same.

I needed to get a handle on my medication therapy. I knew what each of my medications was for, but I wondered if I could eliminate something—anything—of the many drugs I was taking every day. I was still taking the pills that were originally prescribed to me in the hospital, and there had been a few additions and changes by my cardiologist. I was on several blood thinners, medication for my blood pressure and supplements, as well as something for my blood sugar and something for cholesterol. My blood pressure had never been particularly high prior to my cardiac arrest, but the numbers shot up in the hospital after my event and went right back down in the following month. Now, according to the doctors, the idea is to keep my blood pressure low so my heart won't have to work as hard.

The reason I was on so many blood thinners and blood pressure pills was to prevent the blood from clotting in my injured heart during the healing phase. The large number of medications was also prescribed to help my heart pump more easily and to increase my ejection fraction. I knew all of these things, yet I also knew I wanted off some of those medications. If I could only get off of some of those drugs, I knew that progress could be made and I would improve. Besides, medications are very expensive. I wanted another look at my medication therapy.

With a change in cardiologist, I became better informed about my ejection fraction, and I was able to stop taking some of the medications and change some others. I also learned that ACTOS takes three months to take full effect for diabetes. When the ACTOS finally did kick in and my blood sugars stabilized, a significant improvement resulted. I also was able to take a blood pressure medication at a lower dose that didn't make me feel like I was going to faint and collapse at the end of every day. With dogged determination, my family physician worked diligently to get my cholesterol in line. He seemed to have a personal mission to help get things in line for me. He diligently reviewed my medications and changed them as needed. He can also be credited with working to get my blood sugars in line. He genuinely seemed to care.

My wife and I felt as though we needed some time for ourselves. We had devoted so much time and attention to babysitting and household chores and my travel that we didn't do anything for the romantic or spiritual development of our relationship. We began to go out to dinner one night a week. That dinner out once a week became one of my fish dinner nights. The fish just seemed to taste better when I ordered from a restaurant. I just made sure to tell them not to put butter or any additives on my dinner.

For three months after my sudden cardiac arrest, I was not up to any kind of sexual activity. First of all my medication and lowered blood pressure affected the natural hydraulic dynamics of my body. Second of all, I was pretty moody and probably not the best person to be around at that time. Marilyn and I made a few feeble attempts during these first five months but now, I found yet another thing to put on my list as things we definitely needed to work on.

As far as my long-term strategy goes, I have been fortunate enough to find a different job with some great people, which happened to be close to home, so I don't travel as much now. I still work with car dealers by encouraging them to improve their customer service, thus increasing their business. Someone once told me that my work was guaranteed. I'm not jaded enough to believe that, though, because my experience has been that most car dealers are devoted to taking excellent care of their customers.

After I made my lists and changes, I still needed more work on the "fire" part of my survival. I needed to light a fire beneath my motivation. Connecting with other survivors, hearing their stories and yielding to their support was the final step to help heal me.

Every heart patient must overcome the things I describe in this chapter. Some people handle these situations better than others but most of us must find a way to cope with the many changes that have so dramatically changed our lives. In my case, I was coping with survival.

4

Connecting With Other Survivors

In September of 2006, I was contacted by the Minnesota Sudden Cardiac Arrest Survivors Support Group. Since my cardiac arrest occurred in Minnesota and I was taken to an Allina Hospital, my name was supplied to the Minnesota Sudden Cardiac Arrest Support Group. They contacted me shortly after I returned to Overland Park, Kansas. I gave them permission to continue to contact me by e-mail. I would read the minutes from their meetings and read some of the stories, but I didn't really think too much about getting involved. They were in Minnesota and I was in Kansas. Frankly, I really didn't think anyone else felt the way I did anyway.

I had made a personal challenge to work out my heart problems by myself. I was going through this personal tug of war with my medications, exercise routine and eating habits. Visits to my doctors confirmed that I began to improve but would have permanent loss of about 12% of my heart. My ejection fraction improved to 40%, which is good. Marilyn and I had strengthened our relationship and I got along better with just about everyone else. I still had problems with rude people but I seemed to handle situations better.

In August I received an e-mail and a follow-up phone call from Michelle, who was one of the members of the Rochester, Minnesota Survivors group. She invited me to a survivors' conference in Minnesota where, after dinner, there would be other survivors willing to share their stories. The members of the support group were all aware of my dramatic rescue on an airplane. The group even offered to pay for a hotel room for my wife and me.

At the time, the thought seemed kind of bazaar, to drive or fly all of the way to Minnesota just to meet other sick people. The more I thought about going, the more I began to warm to the idea. Marilyn and I had lived in Minnesota years ago and really liked the place. September is a good time to go with the leaves changing, so Marilyn and I discussed the idea, and I called them back to learn more. The group invited me to be the guest speaker and, ultimately, decided to feature my story after the evening dinner. It doesn't take much to flatter me, so I told them we would attend.

Attending the conference was the second life-changing event that occurred in 2006. The first, of course, was my Sudden Cardiac Arrest; the second was meeting and sharing time with the incredible collection of people at the conference.

This survivor's conference featured lectures and workshops for members of the medical and rescue community. There were doctors and nurses from emergency rooms and heart hospitals from all over Minnesota and Wisconsin. Among the attendees were emergency first responders from hospitals, sheriffs department personnel, police departments and ambulance services. Vendors like Medtronic and Zoll were there, Boston Scientific and the American Heart Association, along with many other medical organizations had booths. The Allina Medical organization and Abbott Northwestern Hospital were there to meet and greet the public and welcome me back. What made this event special for me, however, the survivors were there as well, about forty of them.

The opening speech at the conference that day was given by the Coon Rapids County Medical Examiner, Dr. Janis Amatuzio. She spoke about "the things that you know to be true" about life and death. Dr. Amatuzio shared a collection of stories from people who have had a loved one visit them either before or after a recent passing. Her stories bore right to the heart of the death experience. She has written books on the subject of life and death. In her books *Forever Ours* and *Beyond Knowing*, she writes about how we face death and what other people faced when loved ones passed away.

I listened to these heart-wrenching stories of loved ones who had been touched in some way by those they cared about, and her message tore right into my very being. I was visibly shaken. That lecture was the first time I had come to grips with my feelings concerning my survival. In fact, this was the first time I had actually come face to face with my mortality since I returned from the other side.

I had been carrying around the 500 pound gorilla on my back of my survival and the experience I had with God on the other side. I had no one to share any of this. I did not think it was possible that anyone else could possibly understand what I had experienced.

After Dr. Amatuzio's presentation, I had the opportunity to meet her. She has a magnetic personality and is very warm and charming. She seemed to sense my need to vent the emotions bubbling within me concerning my survival. She even told me as much. Her keen insight into the death experience provided an important starting point for me in my emotional healing process. I felt so awed by her presentation–she had really struck a chord within me. She really seemed to get it…she actually understood this death thing. She understood what I was feeling at the time. I asked her how she knew. She was compassionate and looked into my tearful eyes and said *"these were things that we all knew to be true."* This shook me because this is a lesson that I had heard on "the other side" when I had died.

She's a great listener and has met with a great many people who've had close encounters with death. Her book *Beyond Knowing* addressed many of these experiences. Tears streamed down my face as I spoke to her. Even today she continues to be an inspiration to me. This was my first connection that someone else actually understood what I was experiencing.

Later that day, I had the incredible opportunity to meet all forty of the other Sudden Cardiac Arrest survivors. I listened to each story and felt such a keen understanding of what they had each experienced. As I met each person, I felt as though we all held a special bond, tied together not only by the common experience of a Sudden Cardiac Arrest, but also by the knowledge that each of us had died and returned from the other side.

Before I agreed to come to the Minnesota Sudden Cardiac Arrest Summit, I asked if I could invite the people who had a hand in my rescue on the airplane that cold day in January. My rescuers were eagerly welcomed to the conference, so I sent e-mails and made phone calls to each of my rescuers. One lived in eastern Tennessee, another in New Jersey. The two flight attendants lived in Minnesota and they had flight schedules that conflicted. Finally, everyone was able to change their plans, and they all agreed to come to Bloomington, Minnesota for the reunion. I was notified that not only would my airplane rescuers be on hand, but the EMTs who transported me to the hospital would also be there. The Abbott Northwestern Hospital emergency room staff and physicians involved with my rescue had also agreed to be at the medical conference and at the dinner that evening. What an incredible convergence of my universe!

I experienced a magical evening. In attendance at the dinner were medical professionals from hospitals and emergency facilities from all over the state of Minnesota. All of the Sudden Cardiac Arrest survivors and their families were there too. My four angels (rescuers) from the airplane, the three amigos (the EMT's), Linda from the emergency room at Abbott Northwestern Hospital, the nurse who held my hand and told me that I would not have to go through my angioplasty alone, was there. The doctors who were in the emergency room and placed my stent, Drs. Peterson and Wang were there, along with an army of other support staff that had a hand in my rescue that day.

The evening started out with a news clip that I brought from the Fox News interview announcing my emergency rescue and the rapid response to Abbott Northwestern. I opened my story by telling how I had trekked through the Minneapolis airport and how I had collapsed on the plane. I introduced each of my airplane rescuers and my EMT staff. Dr. Peterson then took the lectern and put up a video feed of my heart before the blockage was cleared and a video of the blood flowing freely after my stent placement. The pictures and slides were incredible! I had never seen them before. He also reviewed statistics of Sudden Cardiac Arrest survival. He went on to describe just what happens during a Sudden Cardiac Arrest, that a Sudden Cardiac Arrest is not just a heart attack. He provided an excellent overview of the medical procedures used in my case and how other patients are served with the use if an Implantable Cardio Defibrillator (ICD). He introduced the Abbott Northwestern personnel that were on hand that evening.

I wrapped up the evening with some final comments concerning my recovery. When I was done, the room erupted into applause and cheers. Everyone stood up. All of the other survivors were invited to the front of the room. A huge birthday cake was brought out and presented to all of us on behalf of the Allina Medical organization by Dr. Lick to represent our rebirths into the world. The survivors and their families hugged each other and we even shed a few tears. Photographs captured the occasion and we finally went our separate ways. That night, we each took a little piece of one another home with us in what was left of our hearts.

That evening, I came home with a new mission–to recreate a Sudden Cardiac Arrest Survivors' group in the Kansas City area. After returning home I sprung into action setting up a web site at www.hoascasurvivor.org. I founded a survivors club, and got busy. Local hospitals opened their doors to me to help spread the word, including the honor of being a guest speaker at some local medical programs. Now, as I tell my story and I work to connect with other survivors so they don't have to feel that they're going through the survivor experience alone.

While I had received excellent medical attention from the hospital and doctors, the hardest part of my survival was coping with the many changes I had to face after my event–first as a heart victim and, secondly, as a Sudden Cardiac Arrest survivor. There was no one to talk to who could really understand what I was going through for the longest time. I really did not begin to heal myself until I took a trip to Minnesota to meet and share experiences with a group of fellow survivors.

In some way, I hope the message in my book will reach out to medical professionals, heart patients, heart patients with ICD's and those who have had a Sudden Cardiac Arrest to let them know they're not alone…that there are many others who have experienced what they have experienced. Surviving Sudden Cardiac Death is not an easy thing to deal with. Survival is not the end. Survival is the beginning of a second chance. Many heart patients and SCA survivors undergo many months of rehabilitation efforts. There are times when they feel that no one can understand their plight. These wonderful people need to come together and share their stories with one other. They need to talk with someone who has gone through a similar event to discuss what they have experienced in their recovery. They need to talk with someone else about the roadblocks and speed bumps to getting well. They need to share time with someone who has been there and really understands. They need a support structure.

In a way, we all need some form of survival training. Work to overcome fear and panic. Be confident of your surroundings and make a plan. We were all born ready to ready to fight and survive. Use those instincts to your advantage. With patience and a plan, you will survive and be prepared to make the lifestyle choices for living a healthier, happier and longer life.

5

Facing Post-Medical Depression

Depression is sneaky—this evil monster can creep right up on you, unnoticed. Some people refer to these feelings as the doldrums. You don't realize what's happening until you've slid right there, smack dab in the middle of them. The feeling is in your gut and in your head. Nothing seems quite right, but you don't know what is causing your feelings. Everything just seems futile.

Doctors will often prescribe medication to address some physical ailment. They measure the performance of their prescription against suspected symptoms. While a specific symptom may be addressed, emotional issues are often overlooked. Depression can occur after a major trauma such as a heart attack, sudden cardiac arrest, or even surgery. These emotional issues are left over after the doctors have done their work. They lay there like pieces of a puzzle that don't fit into any specific medical category. With trauma, changing metabolism, variations in medication therapy, and mere day-to-day life the human condition can undergo dramatic ups and downs. Of course, the ups bring joy, even if we don't always understand why we're feeling good on a particular day, but the downs can really get to us—and not being able to understand why we feel down can easily cause us to slip into depression.

Feelings are a tough thing to talk about for many people, especially men. Talking about the tears streaming down my face in the prior chapter and facing the reality of my mortality was not easy for me. I believe that the reason the topic is so hard to discuss is that we may feel a certain way, but finding the words to express those feelings is difficult for many of us. A feeling of queasiness or a heightened sense of awareness can be an expression of how you feel emotionally, or may come as a result of something you ate, or from a lack of oxygen. How do you express that? Is it gas or is it love?

There are physical and chemical reasons our bodies do what they do to cause us to feel a certain way. We'd like to believe the brain is in charge but, really, our emotions are a combination of the brain and other factors that cause us to feel the way we do.

If you have had a heart attack or a Sudden Cardiac Arrest, your brain may be dealing with the simple fact that you had a major trauma and is trying to work out the details. You are also infusing your body with a battery of chemicals and potions dreamed up by the drug companies to address specific health issues. Finally, while your body is trying to heal itself, you are changing the way you eat and exercise. All of these things are going to have an effect on you. Combine all three of these and you and your body are both going through some serious changes. The question is, how do you deal with these changes?

Soldiers who return from war often experience a condition known as "Post Traumatic Stress Disorder." I had to look that one up. The National Institute of Mental Health website describes Post Traumatic Stress Disorder (PTSD) as:

"An anxiety disorder that can develop after exposure to a terrifying event or ordeal in which grave physical harm occurred or was threatened. Traumatic events that may trigger PTSD include violent personal assaults, natural or human-caused disasters, accidents, or military combat. People with PTSD have persistent frightening thoughts and memories of their ordeal and feel emotionally numb, especially with people they were once close to. They may experience sleep problems, feel detached or numb, or be easily startled."

"Exposure to a terrifying event or ordeal in which grave physical harm occurred." That sounds like a heart attack or worse—Sudden Cardiac Arrest or death. Believe me, a death experience can leave you emotionally numb as well.

I have spoken to many people who have had a Sudden Cardiac Arrest. Most of them have a difficult time dealing with a large variety of emotional issues. Many of them experience many of the same symptoms described by the National Health Institute for Post Traumatic Stress Disorder. Many of these victims are under a great deal of emotional stress to come to terms with the physical condition from which they are trying to recover. While some of these survivors have memory loss and anxiety that is quite serious, some of them are just afraid to go to sleep. Loss of sleep and lack of rest is not a good way to treat a heart condition.

Since I'm not a doctor, I'm not qualified to address clinical issues related to health or personal emotional issues. I'm a victim just like many of you reading this book. I have been there and done that, like you and I can look at these things with the knowledge of first hand experience. I also know that depression is a very real thing to deal with, and every heart patient needs to do just that.

Medical professionals who are skilled to work with depression will often prescribe therapies to deal with a single or specific issue that can be identified in a patient. Unless the connection is made to depression or mood swings related to a recent medical occurrence, the condition can often be overlooked.

Some cardio rehab groups do good work helping a patient cope with his or her feelings. In most cases, the nurses and physical therapy professionals are not equipped to adequately help with people who struggle with depression. They are well meaning folks, but they may not recognize all of the signs of depression. The best they can do is to recommend that you see a psychologist or a psychiatrist for counseling. This may be good advice—if you are willing to listen. In some career circles, getting counseling can be a death sentences–no worse than the heart attack itself. These issues and more may be weighing on a patient's mind.

In my case, I had begun the depression cycle within weeks of returning from my release for the hospital. I did not recognize what was happening to me at first. When I did, I simply did not address my feelings when I should have.

Denial of depression is an area for concern. Just how serious is depression? I flew off the handle at people for the slightest reasons. My excuses to my family and work mates was that I was coping with the ups and downs of diabetes. While this is true, I was also suffering bouts of anger, self recrimination and self doubt. I viewed these feelings as a weakness of character and chose not to address the root causes. Simply stated, I have suffered with bouts of depression since my sudden cardiac arrest. At times I felt like I could find no light at the end of a very long tunnel.

My depression doesn't last. I come up for air from time to time and everything seems just fine. When I have something to look forward to, my attitude improves. I did not seek professional advice. I think people need to. I think those who feel depression don't always feel comfortable enough to just jump right into counseling to address their feelings.

I think first step is to recognize that you are suffering from depression. I didn't. Some days I felt fine–other days I was physically drained with my brain going into overload, and you finding coping difficult. Yet still other days, I feel like I may feel like a gorilla is sitting on my chest. On the good days, I feel like a kid again. Frankly, depression can cause a very frustrating and confusing conundrum: I'm feeling strange; do I seek help or not?

My ups and downs were really quite normal–I just needed to understand them. There were real, physical reasons why I was experiencing the emotional roller coaster ride.

You need to discuss this range of emotions with both your family physician and your cardiologist. I didn't and I paid the price of suffering myself and inflicting injury on those I love. These feelings and the things that are causing them will get in the way of your recovery as sure as an elephant in traffic will slow things down. I found that you need to purge yourself of these feelings by documenting them and presenting them to your physician. They can probably help. Talk to someone, anyone, about what your are going through.

There is an old joke that goes something like this: How many psychologists does it take to change a light bulb? The answer is only one, but the light bulb must really want to change. Well, that may be true for a light bulb, but if you have had a major trauma, like a heart attack or a Sudden Cardiac Arrest, and your body is undergoing a series of major changes, you may need a little more than desire to triumph over your drooping emotional state.

Depression is more than a bit of a downer. Depression is a lowered state of mind marked by sadness, inactivity, difficulty in thinking and concentration, and feelings of dejection. Depression will affect not only how you deal with other people but also how they react to you. Give yourself a break. You didn't ask for any of this, but you can take appropriate action to heal yourself. There is a very strong possibility that your condition may be a result of the many medications you're taking, like in my case.

I have found that a blended balance of spirituality, physical fitness, emotional well-being, and mental attitude to create optimum health is necessary for a healthy heart. I don't always succeed. No matter how you define spirituality, this is a very important part of feeling connected to both this world and the next. You must make your own choices, but prayer is a very important part of my daily routine. Often my prayers are just basic "thanks" for the many blessings I enjoy and every now and then, I pitch a query about my "return to life mission." I only hope I'm able to complete whatever task I was sent back to perform with grace and humility, when the time comes.

I chose to handle my depression poorly. You have a chance to handle yours better when the time comes. I am told eating better, exercising more, and spending more time with other people will help. Your physician may offer some other direction. If you choose counseling there are options available through several county and state agencies, however, I am not sure navigating through government bureaucracy is just what a person with depression needs. You may need to make a few calls and work your way through the labyrinth of government programs, but there are services available to every income level.

Changes in diet, changes in medication dosage—as prescribed by my physician—proper hydration, and good exercise wound up helping me with my depression. I have always been pretty active. I think working in a job that put me into contact with many people also helped.

Share happiness and joy. When you don't feel well you don't feel joyful. Sometimes you need one to get the other. Seek out and find some joy and happiness. Find things that are funny and people who make you laugh. You may have to seek laughter out but, believe me there are people around you who can make that happen. There is joy and happiness in everything. Joy is part of the nature of things, the harmony of life, if you will. War, hunger, and despair abound in this world. We hear these things on the news, on the internet, and even from the pulpit. But if you look, there is also humor and happiness. We have lost the art of making a joke, the simple placement of words that will make others laugh. Believe me, you don't have to be too clever to come up with something funny I do, all the time, with some of the world's worst puns. Make the effort. This is the quickest reward you will ever get for the least amount you invest.

Your first source of information on depression should be your family physician. There are a lot of wonder drugs in the market but keep in mind that drugs may have helped get you into this state, so you may need some patience until you and your physician find the proper medication balance to maintain good health.

There is help available. Depression is nothing to toy with. This condition can ruthlessly root itself into your life and, even worse. Depression can make your heart recovery a lot more strenuous. If you are worried about what family members, your employer, or other people may think about your seeking help, remember this–these other people didn't have the heart attack, heart condition or Sudden Cardiac Arrest—you did. You did this thing alone and you will need to get some help to face the consequences. Part of your recovery and coping with your condition is facing the simple fact that you are going to be doing quite a few things differently from now on. Now, get on with the rest of your life!

6

Coping With Change

To laugh often and much;
To win the respect of intelligent people
and the affection of children;
To earn the appreciation of honest critics
and endure the betrayal of false friends;
To appreciate beauty, to find the best in others;
To leave the world a bit better, whether by healthy
child, a garden patch or a redeemed social condition;
To know even one life has breathed
easier because you have lived.
This is to have succeeded.

The above poem is attributed to Ralph Waldo Emerson and is an adaptation of a poem published in 1905 by Bessie Stanley.

The Bessie Stanley version reads:

"He has achieved success who has lived well, laughed often and loved much; who has gained the respect of the intelligent men and the love of little children; who has filled his niche and accomplished his task; who has left the world better than he found it, whether by an improved poppy, a perfect poem, or a rescued soul; who has never lacked appreciation of earth's beauty or failed to express it; who has always looked for the best in others and given them the best he had; whose life was an inspiration; whose memory a benediction."

Published 11/30/1905 in the Lincoln
(Kansas) Sentinel by Bessie Stanley.

Ralph Waldo Emerson changed Bessie Stanley's poem for poetic purpose. Did he improve on the message Bessie was trying to convey? You be the judge. I chose to write on the subject of change for this book because if you have had a Sudden Cardiac Arrest, you will need to make some life-altering changes. I had to make plenty of adjustments, and they weren't easy. In fact, I'm still adding to my list of personal adjustments in my lifestyle and, honestly, it's very challenging.

To take license and quote a cliché "the only absolute is that there are no absolutes." When I worked for one of the large automobile manufacturers, they kept showing movies to us about mice that were looking for cheese, and they told us that we needed to prepare to be a nimble organization. We had meetings where, as employees, we were told that we had to be nimble and flexible. We never fully understood what that meant. We didn't know whether that meant we might have to pack our bags to move to another city or clean out our desks but we knew that change was eminent whether we wanted it or not. They were moving our cheese.

My Sudden Cardiac Arrest brought on an avalanche of change that I did not expect. I have had to move my cheese so often I thought I was in Green Bay, Wisconsin. Understanding things that are strange and different and knowing that your life may depend on those strange things can bring on enough fear to make your head spin faster than Linda Blair's in *The Exorcist*.

I have had to deal a lot with change in the ever-changing automotive industry. As a result, I conducted a class on the subject. I have included many excerpts form that program to help guide you to recognize what you are dealing with. I am not trying to lecture you on this topic but explaining change to you helps me to deal with the changes I continue to face with my heart condition.

Change is a very important part of our lives, and we need to accept change in order to move forward. Bessie Stanley may not have thought so if she ever saw what Ralph did to her poem, but keep in mind that it's easy to talk about change in others while it's very difficult to accept for ourselves. If you don't believe me, put the book down now and cross your arms. Okay, now cross them the other way. Not easy to do, is it? In fact, this change feels strange and uncomfortable.

Many of us don't want things to be different. The familiar is so comfortable for us, and we want things to remain the way they have been. Unfortunately, things changed for those of us with heart conditions and we need to adapt. We form habits and comfort zones, and we stay within those boundaries. We don't want to leave old habits willingly. If you're like me, you probably had your heart attack or cardiac arrest because of some of the habits you've picked up over the years, sometimes without apparent notice. Some of them were even fun, if I remember correctly.

With a heart condition embrace change is critical—no matter how difficult it may be. Unless you make a commitment to change the way you do things, you may be doomed to an unsatisfactory future.

Let's say for the sake of argument that you really enjoy fast food and smoking. You've had a heart attack and then learn that you have high LDL (bad) cholesterol and low HDL (good) cholesterol. Your doctor tells you that continuing to eat foods that are high in saturated fats will only make your heart condition worse. What are your choices? Well, you can keep doing what you're doing and risk losing your life or you can change your eating behaviors and improve your chances for a longer life. This concept sounds simple but you know better.

I've heard some addicts tell me that life just wouldn't be worth living if they couldn't continue to feed their habit. They've already made their choice for change. They haven't chosen to be nimble.

When I was a much younger man, I smoked cigarettes. Smoking seemed as if it were the thing to do at the time. I smoked into my early thirties. I tried to quit on several occasions but I had smoking triggers, so I would always reach for a cigarette when the urge became too much. Finally, one day, I just decided to go cold turkey and quit while I was sick with the flu. When I could barely keep food down, I knew a cigarette wouldn't be the first thing I reached for. After my flu, I used several oral substitutes like Lifesavers® candy and Trident® gum to satisfy my oral urges. Stopping wasn't easy but eventually I did and I gained about ten pounds for my effort. I never lost any of that extra weight, but I'm smoke-free! For months, even years afterward, I would have a dream in which I would be in a social situation, and I would light a cigarette and inhale that gratifying first drag into my lungs. The first drag from that cigarette would seem very satisfying. Then to my shock and horror, I would realize what I had done and I would feel terrible, break out into a sweat, and wake up. Of course, I had not smoked anything but, at the time but the experience was just so real. To stop smoking was a difficult change for me at the time, but that was a good thing I gave up the cigarettes when I did or I might have had my Sudden Cardiac Arrest a lot sooner than I did.

We are all the same. We resist change because of what we do not know. We are afraid to change. Because of that fear, we often put off what we intend to do. We don't want to change because of the fear of the unknown, our perception of what will happen when we do change that prevents us from taking action.

"Change or Die" is a concept I discovered while I was researching change for the automotive leadership skills workshop I mentioned earlier. This is a fascinating study that makes sense for this book because the focus is on heart patients. "Change or Die" faces the very real specter of change that each of us must address at some point.

In a study conducted by Dr. Dean Ornish, a professor of medicine at the University of California in San Francisco, the theory of "Change or Die" was discussed. Dr. Ornish looked at heart patients who had severely clogged arteries. When they were presented with options for health care like a change in diet and abstinence from smoking with counseling sessions and aerobic exercise for their condition, they actually took the program to heart for the first year. After three years 77% of them went back to the lifestyles that created the clogged arteries and heart conditions in the first place. These patients had been presented with the option to "change or die" by their doctors. In other words, selling fear of death to these patients did not work.

Dr. Ornish then asked these doctors to try to motivate their patients instead, with a new vision of the 'joy of living.' He wanted to convince the patients that they can feel better and not by just live longer but do the things they really wanted to do. This goes to the root that people will do things that make sense to them. Dr. Ornish recommended longer walks, enjoying sex or having more fun with the grandkids. "Joy is a more powerful motivator than fear," Ornish said.

Dr. Edward Miller, the dean of the medical school and CEO of the hospital at Johns Hopkins University, is quoted as saying,

"Many patients could avoid the return of pain and the need to repeat surgery, not to mention arrest the course of their disease before it kills them, by switching to healthier lifestyles. Yet very few do. If you look at people after coronary-artery bypass grafting, two years later, 90% of them have not changed their lifestyle."

Imagine that. We know that the things we do will kill us but we continue to do them even when warned about the outcome.

The decision to change is up to you but several factors must be considered. For my automotive lectures, I address change by presenting a series of steps before a shift in thinking can take place for most people:

- **Fear of Change**: Fear is looking at the unknown and applying your imagination to all of the possibilities, many of them not good. These are generally shaped by perceptions. Albert Einstein said, "Perception is the accumulation of all prior knowledge and experience." This means that perception is simply a state of mind and, as such, can change. The most basic roadblock is to move from what we know to what we don't know. We simply don't want to move from our comfort zone to areas of the unknown.

- **Denial**: It's a lot easier to reject what we hear than to embrace the notion of moving into a new direction or to accept what we know to be the solutions to our dilemmas. Denial is our brain's safety mechanism that wraps us in a false blanket of security. I met a lady in cardio rehab who told me she was Cleopatra and that she was the queen of denial. Cute pun, but she knew her limitations.

- **Bargaining and Negotiating**: Once we have accepted that change is inevitable we begin to bargain to make the pain of change less severe. The child in all of us will play this tug-of-war with reality. I was notified that I was being relocated years ago. The decision had already been made and when I figured this out, I began to negotiate where I would have to go. This soon led to the next step.

- **Anger**: Once we finally realize that our comfort zone, our security nest has been shaken, we become angry and indignant. This is the by-god-I-just-won't-stand-for-it stage. Your mind starts focusing on revenge, and temper tantrums, very real manifestations of anger.

- **Acceptance**: When you finally realize that the change is going to take place regardless, a certain peace sets in, and acceptance comes slowly, and you prepare for the changes you know will happen. This is the settling stage. I remember the car I had to settle on, when I was in high school, instead of the one I really wanted.

In his book *The 7 Habits,* Dr. Steven Covey talks about the paradigm shift. This is the complete and radical movement in belief from one concept to another. We actually make many shifts in our lives. We change our fundamental beliefs both consciously and unconsciously. We go through a shift in thinking as a result of many factors affecting our lives or even an event such as a heart attack.

The choice for personal change is a difficult one. You must be motivated in order to change. What motivates you?

Some people are motivated by money, greed, love, pride, faith, acceptance, desire, fear or even the fear of loosing something they perceive as valuable. Some people are simply motivated by the undeniable power of suggestion.

In order to facilitate change, a clear set of objectives or goals must be recognized. This approach will net the best results. Lifestyle changes will follow with a certain direction. Goals are the agreement you have made with yourself, those that will propel you toward success. Goals are a kind of road map of how to approach that which will lead to your ultimate destination: a happier, healthier, whole YOU.

You need to write your goals down so you can review them often. This enables accountability in the event that we're tempted to change our minds, since having documented goals provides a good reminder. Set a deadline for the completion of your goal and be prepared to make adjustments from time to time. Goals need to be measurable so you know if you are making progress or not. If your goal is a lower LDL and a higher HDL, then measure your results. If your goal is lower blood sugar or blood pressure, then measure your daily results. This is easy enough to do with today's tools. If you are obese, work on your situation incrementally and understand the enabling factors and triggers you have for your weight condition.

Goals also need an action plan. How you will achieve your goal? Think through each step, realistically. Your plan for success needs to make sense before it will work. A goal I have set for myself is to take a brisk three-mile walk each morning. A three-mile walk generally takes me about forty-five minutes, but I try to walk further, perhaps up to sixty minutes. I keep a record, in case I miss my walk. My goal is to exercise forty-five minutes a day for five days a week. I began this exercise plan shortly after returning home from the hospital. I also choose to measure my glucose level twice daily in an effort to keep my overall blood sugar below 120. I record the scores each time I lance my fingers. I record what I eat, and I record what I was doing when my blood sugar soars unusually high or dips too low.

Goals need to be reviewed regularly, because they don't always stay the same. This is another good reason to document them on paper. Remember, the goals you set are for you and no one else. No one will be looking over your shoulder to check on you. Goals are personal and are for your own benefit. This is the bargain you are making with yourself. Don't change because someone else tells you to, you must change for the things in life that you feel that are worth living for. You must change for your own reason, and then you will stick to them. Here are some helpful tips for working toward your goals:

- Brainstorm with your family members and friends on attainable goals.

- List your goals and then prioritize them.

- Itemize the values you are trying to accomplish with each goal. In other words, once you have established a goal like lower blood sugar, determine just what number you are shooting for, establish a value, or where you want to go with the goal, as part of your plan.

- Focus on one goal at a time. The old joke, "How do you eat an elephant?" When I asked my grandson, he said "with ketchup." The real answer, of course, is one piece at a time.

- Set both short-term goals and some "stretch goals" for yourself. These are the big ones—the ones that will take some time to accomplish. One such goal could be completing a college degree. It's never too late! Short-term goals are for now, today, this week this month, this quarter. Stretch goals are for this year, in five years, in ten years, and "before I die." When I was in high school, a study habit I learned was to get the easy stuff done first then get to work on the harder assignments. The task of doing all of the homework became that much easier.

- Personal Goals: Set some goals for personal development, family relationships, and health & welfare. These are critical to your overall state of mind.

- Set goals for items you need or want like a new car, house, boat, or TV.

- Business Goals: Do you have any career choices in mind? What would you really like to be doing? Set the goal and then set about figuring out how to obtain your objective.

- Right now, yes while you are reading this, pick up pen and paper. List two goals that you want to achieve when you finish this book.

"It takes a lot of courage to release the familiar and seemingly secure, to embrace the new. But there is no real security in what is no longer meaningful. There is more security in the adventurous and exciting, for in movement there is life, and in change there is power." Alan Cohen

Change is necessary for improvement in your life. You and no one else must make the decision to do something! You must be committed to the process of change. To quote Don Reed, President of Dealer Pro Training: "Making a commitment is like bacon and eggs, the chicken was involved but the pig was committed."

Surround yourself with others who are as committed as you are. Do not rely on the advice of enablers—those who encourage you to take that one bite of something you know is way too greasy for you to eat or those who insist that skipping two walks this week won't matter. These people don't have your best interests at heart. If you are committed to change, you must find others who are as committed as you to reinforce your motivation. This is not to say those who are enablers are bad people, because most of them are just the opposite, they are often so in love with you that they cannot say no. Be prepared to listen to your inner self and hear the message that reinforces the change you want to occur.

"No person is your friend who demands your silence, or denies your right to grow."
—Alice Walker

"And the day came when the risk to remain tight in a bud was more painful than the risk it took to blossom."
—Anais Nin

"We do not grow absolutely, chronologically, we grow sometimes in one dimension, and not in another; unevenly; we grow partially. We are relative. We are mature in one realm, childish in another. The past, present, and future mingle and pull us backward, forward, or fix us in the present. We are made up of layers, cells, constellations."
—Anais Nin

"If you don't like change, you're going to like irrelevance even less."
—(Chief of Staff, U.S. Army) General Eric Shinseki

Frankly, the choice to change is yours. Find your star in the universe and shoot for it.

7

What is a Healthy Lifestyle?

People often talk about healthy lifestyle changes as if they were talking about changing their shoes. You simply take off this lifestyle and put on another. How difficult can changing lifestyles be? If you are like me you would rather sit through an IRS audit with Attila the Hun than make dramatic changes in the way they live, eat and exercise. Once you've begun your transformation through a personal shift in thinking, and you're ready to try a new lifestyle, you'll have to decide just what that new lifestyle will be. I'm not suggesting you take up with a goat, wear sheepskins, and chant mantras of eternal bliss. If you are looking for that kind of change, you will have to find another book. The kind of lifestyle changes I am talking about are those that the medical community is already telling us we should embrace. These are the ones that will help keep you alive so you can enjoy the wonderful things you have in store for your future. I've broken some of these lifestyle changes down to make them easier for me to understand:

Eating

People are great to instruct other people to "change your diet." If you have favorite foods or if you watch *Emeril*, you know there is something called "comfort food." This is food you are most comfortable eating. This kind of food makes you feel good and you are (temporary) at harmony with the universe while you are eating. For many folks, this could be ice cream, chocolate, pizza, pasta, or even a glass of beer. Comfort can come in anything that makes you feel good while being consumed. Generally, these same comfort foods have caused many of us to fall into the health risk position that we now face. The hard thing is, what do we give up, and how soon?

After my cardiac arrest and subsequent recovery at home, I became a food Nazi. I literally cut everything out of my diet I perceived as being bad for me. I came out of the hospital a full-blown type II diabetic, my cholesterol had spiked, and common sense told me that things like salt and fats were bad for me. I had decided that food was my enemy. I settled on a bland and tasteless diet of very few choices. I lost a few pounds but nothing significant. I was miserable every time I sat down to eat. My wife, bless her soul, did everything she could to comply with my wishes. When I traveled, I had difficulty with the menus, giving more than a fair share of grief to my servers, I'm sure. Most of them were very understanding, and they did their best to find things on the menu they thought I could eat.

I slugged along like this for a couple of months until I finally went to a hospital recommended dietitian. The hospital kept referring to me a professional nutritionist. If only I would've listened sooner! She called our house several times, and I cancelled several appointments before I finally made the visit. I thought she was likely full of good intentions, but I knew she was attached to the hospital, so I didn't consider her program to be anything I would consider relevant. I was not interested in hearing about food pyramids and nutritional buzzwords. I had made up my mind that the austere program that I was subjecting myself to be better than anything anyone could suggest to me. *That would be the arrogance of ignorance.*

First of all, she was pleasant and, yes, she was full of good intentions, but she was determined so she asked a lot of open-ended questions about what I was doing and how. She did go through the basics with me but did not dwell on them. Instead, we focused on food trade-offs. These are things you can do with your diet or food plan to trade one thing for another. Weight Watchers® has known about this stuff for years, but the thought of measuring everything I ate on a scale and keeping strict records was just more than I could handle. Weight Watchers® is a great program, but as with all goals, you have to plan your work and stick with the plan in order to work.

Trade-off's do work if you are conscious of what you are trading. You cannot trade salad for a couple of pork chops and a six-pack of beer, for example. If you know you are going to have a cookie, you will trade something else in your food plan for that day to account for the calories in the cookie. The dietician convinced me that if I continued the way I was going, I would probably drop the food plan I had set up for myself all together for less healthy choices and more dire consequences.

The most important lesson the dietician taught me was how to find healthy nutrition—and she taught me with out the use of a pyramid. I found that you do need to keep balance in a healthy diet. The problem is that most of us have not kept balance in our diets for years. We have relied on the comfort food factor too much. The dietician's point was that while I made a pretty good choice to give up the eggs due to cholesterol, I should also consider occasionally eating a slice of bacon for the protein. I just thought that bacon had so much fat and wouldn't be a good choice and so I shouldn't eat any bacon at all. The key word to keep in mind is *balance*. She said that an egg now and then is probably okay but not daily and definitely not a bunch of fried eggs. French fries would not be a good substitute for a baked potato without butter, yet a sweet potato with no additives is better than a white potato with no butter.

The dietician told me that you need a balance of proteins, fats, carbohydrates, minerals, vitamins, water, and roughage in my diet. Depending upon a person's weight and exercise regimen, the percentage of each will vary with every individual. If the current diet is coke and pizza, a few changes may have to be made.

America is obese. This revelation is more than a statistical fact. All you have to do is go to the grocery store, the movies, or the mall, and take a look at the people around you. We got fat because our culture has made allowances for itself. We tend to fool ourselves into believing we "deserve what ever we want" or "just this one time" or even "greed is good." We live in a very selfish society. This is exhibited by the foods we eat, and in many of our lifestyle choices. I must constantly be challenging myself so I do not become another sedentary and non-active couch potato.

How do we change? We got to this place but we don't have to stay here. Changing is much easier said than done, for most people. Let's start with a little education:

The Three Basic Food Groups: Salt, Sugar, and Fat

The great satire writer Erma Bombeck came up with salt, sugar, and fat as the three basic food groups. She came up with an upside-down pyramid. This pyramid is not the good food pyramid that most nutritionists use; this is the pyramid that most Americans live with. The unfortunate fact is that most people in America need their daily ration of salt, sugar, and fat in order to get through another day. We may all think this is true, but too many days of eating from those food groups, and we won't have to worry about surviving any days at all.

Many people I talk to think about the foods they love and what they will miss if they have to give any of them up. That is certainly one way to live, but more importantly, we should be focusing on the things we are missing out on, if we don't embrace a healthier lifestyle. What about that vacation we had planned, the beach or the long walks in the mountains? What about love and sex and feeling good about ourselves? What about all of the things we are missing out on. Generally, all of that comes with eating a more healthy diet. It's true—when you begin to eat better, you'll feel better and your will to do more things will increase. This is absolute science, folks, and I'll find a reference somewhere. Oh yeah…my grandmother says so.

Years ago, when I was very young and my grandmother was still with me, she would tell me that if I was feeling a little depressed I should flush my system out with water. What she would tell me to do was drink several glasses of water a day for a while and, soon, I would feel much better. Actually, she was just telling me to hydrate my body. This is something most of us do not think about on a daily basis. Hydration does work, and is good for healthy balance in your body. Anywhere you go, you will hear that you should drink eight glasses of water a day. That is a lot of water and a lot of trips to the restroom but that is the idea. We are flushing out the excess salts and minerals that the body does not need. This is a good thing, and that leads us to salt.

Salt

Salt was used for millennia as a form of money. The acid flavor of salt really makes stuff taste good. Salt is everywhere with phrases that permeate our culture, like; "She was the salt of the earth," or "Lot's wife turned into a pillar of salt." "Time to get back to the salt mine" as a metaphor for work, and they say that "athletes and marathon runners need to take salt tablets." Yet on the opposite side of the spectrum, we don't want to "rub salt into the wound," for "we are as alike as salt and pepper." Jewish tradition referred to Mosaic law as the "salt and light." Even the word "salary" comes from salt as a way to get paid in salt. Salt has become very ingrained into our social structure and language. The Salt Institute (there actually is such a thing and you can find them online) will tell you that salt is actually good for you—and salt is—in moderation.

I have a personal choice to put no additional salt on my food. I feel that I get enough salt in all of the foods that are served to me. Salt is possibly one of the leading enemies of people who have hardening of the arteries. The Salt Institute would disagree with me. They feel there is an ongoing controversy on the subject. You will have to make your own choices, but keep this in mind: if you read the food labels on all processed food, as I do, and look for the sodium (salt) content, you will see a significant quantity of salt in just about everything you buy. Even a simple can of green beans has a load of salt, unless you look for the unsalted type.

Salt is everywhere, in almost everything you touch as food. While at the airport the other day, a co-worker pointed out that the Healthy Caesar Salad had over 2,000 grams of salt on the label. Wow! We have the ancient Egyptians beat; all you have to do is go to the store and buy a shelf load of processed foods and pack your body in them when you go. You will be preserved for eternity, even if you do smell a little like hamburger helper, you'll look good.

Sugar

We love sweet things in our lives. We like to "sweeten the deal." Former TV sitcom star Jackie Gleason used to say, "How sweet it is," "Keep your words soft and sweet, because you may have to eat them someday," and "Like a kid in a candy shop." If it tastes so good, how could it be so bad? The bad all comes down to a disruptive little organ called the pancreas and an imbalance of sugar in the bloodstream—either too much or too little. You can become either Type I or a Type II diabetic. There are lots of reasons someone can become diabetic, but with sugar, it's not the road trip that will kill you; it's the destination.

Many people who are diabetic have inherited the trait. Diabetes can creep up on you before you are aware. In my family, heart disease is almost unknown. Most of my uncles and aunts have succumbed to the fatal diabetes. I am now a diabetic, and I measure my blood sugar twice a day. Before my cardiac arrest, I had slightly elevated blood sugar. My doctors advised me that while I was not quite diabetic and I did not need medication, I should watch my diet. After my cardiac arrest, my blood sugar shot through the roof. I use medication, diet, and exercise now to keep my blood sugars under control.

I try to avoid processed sugar in all forms. This is difficult to do because sugar is added to a lot of foods. As with salt, you really must read the labels to see what you are getting. I also really enjoy foods like bread, beer, pasta, sweet tea, pineapple, and the list goes on. The problem is that my body turns all of that stuff into sugars that I can't process in my pancreas.

After Sudden Cardiac Arrest, many people start out, as I did, with a rigid diet and draconian food choices. This choice will put you at risk of doing exactly what you shouldn't do and, that is, dropping the diet plan. All at once, that pizza looks good, so you think just this one time won't hurt anything, right? Then the one time becomes a pattern, and then a habit, and then you are in worse shape than before you began and your body just can't adjust.

Diabetics have a tough time because of the swings in the body's response to sugar. Blood sugar can go up and down often without any discernable reason. The rise and fall of blood sugars affects my mood. These fluctuations in blood sugar affected my physical stamina and, consequently, affected my whole outlook on life. Sometimes I just become listless and weak. Sometimes I become moody and say things I don't really mean. I was a football player, racquetball player, and skier who had been in fairly good condition for most of my life. Diabetes changes things; diabetes can bring you to your knees.

Even with medication, diabetes is a roller coaster ride. You can't control diabetes with food, either, but what you eat will definitely alter how you feel. I know people who have forgotten to take the medication or they got no physical exercise because of a physical disability. They have incredible swings in their ability to process sugar. Their moods and physical condition are like a pendulum, constantly moving.

Don't let anybody kid you diabetes is a dogfight. Diabetes is the toughest thing I live with, and struggle to control. I have family members who take insulin. They watch what they eat and exercise and, still, they have ups and downs. If your doctor tells you that you have a blood sugar problem, now is not too soon to exercise and watch your diet. If, later on, you need the medication or insulin, then you are two-thirds of the way to living with a manageable disease.

Fat

Fat the third side of the upside-down food pyramid. Fat is the stuff that generally makes food taste good. You can't make a cake without fat of some kind and fat is in just about every fast food and snack you buy. Doctors will tell you that fat, along with salt, are major contributors to cholesterol and arteriosclerosis, or hardening of the arteries.

I lived in the south for many years. My greatest joy of living there was the food. This food is fantastic! Everything I love: fried chicken, catfish, Cajun red beans and rice, jambalaya, sweet tea, fritters, bread pudding, corn on the cob dripping with sweet butter, cornbread with butter and honey, blackened red fish seared in lard, in a 1400° skillet, fried oyster po-boys with french fries, and anything with a sauce or gravy was outstanding. I ate this great food only occasionally, good thing too, because unchecked, I would've been as big as a shopping mall.

I have high cholesterol. I take medication, and with doctor supervision, I now have my cholesterol count under control. I don't eat all of the wonderful things I love to eat. I may eat some of those things now and then when I trade one food for another. Some things for me are simply to be avoided. I read somewhere that if you slip and eat just one meal of fast a food hamburgers and greasy french fries, you've just wiped out all of your dietary effort and must start all over again. I don't know if that's true or not, but I do know that some foods for me are just not to be eaten. You will have to make your own choices, in consultation with your doctor and your dietician. A diet must be workable and the key word here is sustainable—anything else, you won't stick with the plan.

Balance is important and your body needs fat—the good kind. You'll find this in Omega^3 foods like fish and in nuts like walnuts and in flaxseed. Where the heck do you find flax? Isn't that what the miller's daughter wove into gold for the manikin, Rumpelstiltzkin? Seeds are available for purchase in some grocery stores, and they're available in farmer's markets and many natural food stores as well. They can be added to salads, breads, breakfast cereals, and more. I am told that if you take 1000 mg of Omega^3 tablets and eat fish several times a week, you will do better than you probably are doing now. Just stay away from processed meats, fried pork rinds, fat on steak, and such. I definitely don't recommend the bacon double cheeseburger with all of the condiments.

No matter what you may read from the Cheese Institute, cheese is fat—and fat will break down into cholesterol in your blood stream. *Man, I love cheese, too.* Cheese is the food product that kept those silly little mice wondering; who moved their cheese? Cheese is as sacred as Mother and apple pie—cheese is the only way I would eat broccoli for years. Now, I just eat the broccoli. Discuss cheese with your dietician. There are low-fat cheddar cheeses out there that are delicious. In moderation, you might be able to slip cheese as well as other foods you like into your diet.

So now you have the upside down three basic food groups. Salt, sugar, and fat are the cocktails that will clog your arteries and stop your heart. Life choices like smoking, taking recreational drugs, over-medicating on prescription drugs, or alcohol can open the door to an early cardiac arrest as well. Most importantly, read the labels on everything you buy. Look for the fat content, the cholesterol, the sodium, phosphates, and the sugars. Everything you need to know is generally printed on the label, the Food and Drug Administration (FDA) requires this posting. All you have to do is take the time to read the label.

Some people really believe that if they go to a nutrition store and pick out an armload of vitamins and minerals that make sense to them, that they will be healthier and happier. "Of course these vitamins and minerals work, the bottle says so," I have heard people say. The simple fact is that food supplements and vitamin abuse will lead to drastic imbalances in your body's ability to function properly. There is a whole industry that supports the use of nutritional additives, vitamins, and minerals to a better life. Many of them are great and they may do good things for you, but my only admonition is to consult your family physician with whatever you plan to ingest. What you may consider to be a good idea may very well have life or death consequences. Choices like this could be another way to earn yourself a cardiac arrest. Don't take the ads at face value. Get a second opinion, ask your doctor.

Exercise

This is the lifestyle choice that gets to most people. "Yeah, I can give up that side of beef now and then, but you want me to what?" Many people put exercising right up there with the Spanish Inquisition. Exercising is just basic physics. How do you get a body at rest into motion? Inertia is that funny word that means to get moving.

The thought of dying might get you moving faster than the motivation to follow a TV exercise program. Exercise, like diet, must be sustainable. I know several people that equate exercise with running. They see these lithe fit runners with their six-packs as they trot down the street. *Man, to be like that.* But the reality for most everyday folks is they might go out and run, and then they pull a muscle or even injure themselves worse. Running is not for everyone. In my case, I do a power walk most mornings with my dog. I am not ready to run; I might jog something loose that I don't want to lose.

Begin an exercise program that is right for you. At cardio rehab, I saw many caregivers introduce exercise regimens to patients who wouldn't have known how to begin otherwise. They taught me to begin slowly. My best advice to you is to get a trainer, if at all possible. This may mean joining a health club, going to the YMCA/YWCA, or looking into a community health program. My cardiologist recommends this to me every time I see him. *What would my dog, Faye, do if I didn't walk with her that three to four miles every morning?* I am, however, looking into several health clubs as I write this.

Doctors and medical experts everywhere agree that you need a minimum of forty minutes of exercise. You need to elevate your blood pressure and heart rate in order to burn calories and to keep yourself healthy. Just keep in mind that twenty minutes is too short for an exercise program. I feel you need to exercise four to five times a week to make any difference in your physical condition. In the wintertime, you can even walk inside the mall, but I do suggest leaving your pocketbook at home. Too many stops can become expensive.

If you have not been exercising regularly up to this point, getting started may be a rough choice for you. Recruit a friend, join a club, or walk someone's dog for them. Make the commitment. Exercise will also help get your blood pressure and diabetes under control.

What if you were suddenly faced with a life-or-death situation? What if you were told you could live but, in order to live, you had to take a bunch of drugs, exercise a lot, and change the way you eat—perhaps eliminating your favorite foods? To complicate things, what if you smoked, were obese, and/or liked to tip a few? Could you, would you, change—if your life depended on change? There are no perfect solutions. Accept the changes you need to make in your life. Remember, you must take everything you do in moderation, and with a liberal dose of love. That's my formula for a healthy lifestyle. I was told this sounds too much like Dr. Phil, but you know, I believe that looking forward and planning ahead works.

8

Making the Most of Your Second Chance

"If I could live my life over again, I would do things differently." Perhaps you have said that yourself. Is it true? What exactly would you do differently? Everyone who has had a Sudden Cardiac Arrest has died. Those of us who died have all come back with the opportunity to do something differently. We can make a difference: we can make changes in our lives and in the lives of others, if we choose to do so. The only thing holding us back is ourselves.

Several people have asked me if my sudden cardiac arrest has caused me to do anything differently. I think that in those months following my return from death that I was pretty self-absorbed. I was focused on myself a lot. Feeling better and getting back to work were priorities. It took time and a lot of long walks to come to the conclusion that I was simply a different person from the one who stepped on that airplane in January.

At first I was wrapped up in self-pity and aggravation over how I felt. Both medication and diet had an affect on my general well being and outlook. I did not feel blessed, lucky or the recipient of any great miracle. I came to realize that my event was more than a heart attack. I had suffered from a Sudden Cardiac Arrest, died and returned to the living. I know that I was sent back for reasons that are yet to unfold. I began to become aware of the changes taking place in me.

I took a look at the world around me, I saw that I needed to focus less on what others were doing that irritated me, and instead focus more on what simple tasks I could perform for other people. These tasks could be simple things like picking up after other people and not thinking about it or letting a person turn in front of me while I was driving. Time had to become less important, and deeds of every kind have become more important.

What I have discovered is that I am not in a footrace with death. Whatever I must do while I am here on earth, I will do in whatever time I am allotted. In my opinion, it is supremely important that a person enjoy the view and the ride while you are in the car. After you get to the destination, it is too late. The impression I got while I was on the other side was that our main purpose on earth is to help other people traverse through life and be good custodians of the world around us. It is not easy making it from day to day and it is a whole lot harder for some people than others. Each of us can do a little bit to make the others' journey a bit easier.

A month or two after I came home, I began to chronicle the events of my sudden cardiac arrest, as I remembered them. Eventually, when I was contacted by the Minnesota support group, I began to feel like something indeed special had happened to me.

You see, when I retuned home from the hospital, the constant feeling that I had unfinished business weighed heavily on me. I kept asking God to give me at least a hint. I probably received several but was too dense to realize what was in front of me. When I returned home from Minnesota after the survivors' conference I was convinced that I needed to tell the world about Sudden Cardiac death.

I became galvanized in my convictions to help inform the public, form a local support group in the Kansas City area and save lives. I also began to take a second look at the people around me and what I needed to do to make order out of what I had perceived as chaos when I died.

Deep inside, I felt that my return to the living had a lot to do with my grandchildren and what influence I might have on them as they develop and grow. So, in my case, my first task was to re-establish a relationship with my family. In my effort to provide for them and worry about my health, I had alienated just about everyone.

I work with my family and their needs as each day unfolds. The difference is how I feel about my family members and my commitment to listen to them a little closer. Each member of my family has some special need from me. I just need to be alert enough to detect what that need is and then respond appropriately. I miss the mark from time to time but my perspective is to try harder than I ever have in my life. I am using my second chance to handle things a little differently with each of them.

I have also made it a point to reach out to other people, people I do not know. It seems that I am able to connect with more people in a more meaningful way than ever before. Perhaps I am just paying more attention but I do feel that I can help people along every opportunity I get. I began to take another look at the world around me. Instead of thinking about the reason I returned to earth to perform some unknown task, I began to think about what I could do each day for just about anyone I met.

I have read things recently like "God wants us to make money; it is His money and we can use it to do the things he wants us to do for ourselves." That is a very selfish kind of thinking that is not, in my opinion, in the master plan for us while we are here. In my experience, I doubt if God thinks very much about money or the things you can buy with it. When you go onto the other side, you definitely leave everything behind. I am also not an advocate of giving your worldly possession all away and moving into a com-mune to chant rhythmic hymns. Not that giving money away and chanting rhythmically would be all that bad, but it's just not for me. I believe in working hard and using what I earn to benefit those in my family first and then other people, as I see fit. This is my choice. You may choose differently.

I also believe that it is important to give of myself—to give my time and attention to helping people as often as I can. I do this in my life and I do this in my work. I help people in their businesses. I choose to talk to the public about the nature of Sudden Cardiac Arrest and what can be done to prevent Sudden Cardiac Death. I talk to inspire others into action. I choose to volunteer my time with a variety of public service programs. I do what I can when I can. I tell you this because these are my choices and I have always believed in leading by example. You can do the same.

Has my life changed since I have returned from the dead? I have given more of myself to others since my return to this life because I feel that it's part of our true mission here on earth. I am not committing myself to a life of poverty and charity, and I am not doing it to feel good. I just want to attempt to make someone else feel better or feel good about him or herself and make this part of my daily lifestyle. Do I mess up and say something inappropriate or lose my temper from time to time? Yeah, guilty as charged! After all, I am trying to cope with the weird chemistry I am stuck with, but I do ask for forgiveness and move on, making the next day a little better for someone else. I have to make a constant effort.

As you read this, you will make your own choices about what direction you will take with your own life. One thing is for certain–you can begin to focus more on others and less on yourself today, right now, at the moment of reading this paragraph. You do not need to wait. Take the responsibility of worrying about yourself off of your shoulders. This is the first step in developing a more positive self-image. You can think about what simple task you can perform for someone else.

If you do something for someone, do so selflessly. Your reward will be the smile or the appreciation you receive from the helping hand. That do unto others thing, transcends all religious beliefs and cultures, you know. Do you think that's a coincidence?

Each day, I now ask myself, "What opportunities lie in front of me today? What can I accomplish?" In order to understand this, I start each day with a list. It is critical that I organize things in my cluttered mind so I know where I should start first. Making lists and getting organized is right at the top of my priorities on how to make life a happier place.

I have made my choices for my second chance at life, what about you? Making the most of your second chance may have more challenges than mine. I expect there will be readers of this book who have had severe heart conditions and lost much more of their heart than I did. If you have a genetically related heart condition and you are just now coming to grips with life altering changes, your second chances will reflect your new perspective. If you have an implantable cardio defibrillator (ICD) you will be making changes in your lives within the limitations of your mechanical devices. The purpose of this chapter is to look beyond your personal limitations and reach out to other people at every opportunity.

If you or a family member has survived a heart attack, Sudden Cardiac Arrest or an ICD, then you are going to be worried about physical limitations. We have always been faced with limitations, haven't we? Our parents set limits in what we could do and when we could do it. We had limitations in school and at work concerning our behavior. Now, our limitations may be money, opportunity and, now, possibly even physical limitations. As a result, over the years, we have simply coped with our limitations.

Your second chance is your opportunity to make real change. Your physician will help you figure out some of your physical limitations and how to work within their boundaries. You will make the choice on how you will use your assets. What is it that will really make your life more worthwhile? What do you like to do? What are your secret ambitions? How can you touch the moon?

Be honest about your feelings. You need to be honest with yourself first, and then you can be honest with other people. If you are lying to yourself about your condition or situation, you will not provide a template for change. I know addicts. I have had them in my family. Addictive behavior is based on lying first to yourself then to everyone else. They lie because they are committed to their addiction. I believe the first step is to admit the addictive behavior and then act to facilitate change. In my opinion, honesty is a pure belief that there is no deception to what you say or do. Your second chance allows you the opportunity to live an honorable second life. Look at everything with renewed clarity and note the differences. You will be surprised by the number of options that you have.

Perhaps your ambition is to take a cruise that you have dreamed of taking but never felt that you could, or should, take. What about that art course you have often thought about taking? You could be going to ball games again. What is your personal ambition? For some people just being healthy enough to take a long walk, enjoy sex with your special someone, play eighteen holes of golf or is it just feel good again is what they desire and miss the most from their lives. When your doctor places lifestyle choices in front of you to "change or die," the message is pretty clear, that smoking is not healthy or you need to lose weight. On the other hand maybe you need to think hard about the things you miss, the things that you really want in life, what is important to you and then take some action that will get you where you want to be. Action can be incremental. It does not have to take place all at once. What was the old saying that I mentioned earlier in the book? "How do you eat an elephant? One bite at a time." Or was that an eggplant? Either way, for me it would take me a long time to eat either.

If you are obese and have physical limitations or perhaps have been a life-long smoker, your choices may seem more difficult. I have lived around obese people my whole life. There is a great challenge in store for anyone who wants to alter an obese lifestyle—but it can be done. Life is full of trade-offs. If you chose to make some changes in your lifestyle in order to do some of the things that you really feel are important, then you will be making the most of your second chance.

If you have not had a heart attack or a cardiac arrest and you are reading this book, the same choices are open to everyone. It does not matter what your religious affiliations is, or your race, or your political beliefs or social standing, you do not need to die to have a reason to change the way you look at life and take a new look at others living it. Begin to look at life and what your choices would be if you were to change the way you do things.

I don't know how you can make the most of your second chance but everyone can improve relationships with those who mean the most to them. It is never too late to say "I love you" or "I truly care." Instead of getting angry with your children, it might be better to simply take stock, stop, and listen again and take a new approach. Children don't always remember all of the hugs they got but they sure remember the punishment they received. Let your children know that you love them. When you are gone, it is too late. Instill in them the value of family.

Acquaintances do come and go and I can tell you that, in the end, only family remains and only family matters. You will develop friendships in your life that become, in a sense, family. They are the same. So, nurture relationships for family and friends with your second chance. Value those friendships as well as your parents, siblings, and children. You can never underrate what you say or do in their eyes and in their minds. It may be more profound than you think. So regard them highly and express your love to them in this life often. It's important for both of you that you do so.

According to my son, the harmony of life is measured by the music you listen to. There may be something to that. Music is mathematical in nature, and it somehow moves each human in its own special way. Some people dance or tap out the rhythm, while others feel the need to burst into vocal chorus. The heart is a rhythm instrument. It is important to keep it in tune. Music, in some way, helps to soothe that ailing heart and keep it in rhythm. I strongly urge readers of this book to spend a little time each day listening to the rhythms that help keep them in sync with their inner feelings.

One thing I have discovered with my second chance is that as human beings, we must be responsible custodians for our behavior and our place on earth. You must accept change in your life, make a commitment to make a difference, and even commit to making a list. Start with the easiest thing to do first. Respect the life and space of other humans.

A second chance can start today. You can make a positive difference in one other person's life. Take the time to make that phone call, text message, e-mail, special recognition, compliment or just a smile and reach out to someone else and let him or her know that they too matter in this world. This will do a world of good for both of you.

Once you make the changes you need to make in your life, you will release an incredible amount of energy. In the scheme of things, the boss that you believe who does not have your best interests at heart, the customers who are always angry and impolite, the rude drivers, the hostile spouse, if you think about it these are things that really do not matter. They seem important at the time but if you focus your energy on these feelings, they will have control over you. Once you let them go you will realize that their negative force will have less influence over you. Use what you know of yourself to reach out to someone else to improve someone else's life. Do this at every opportunity, and the negative feelings will not have control over you.

I have returned to life with a second chance to make a difference in the way I live and the way I can help others to live. I see my second chance as a way to do things a bit differently than I did the first time around. After all, what good is a second chance if you simply repeat the mistakes you made the first time around? Making the most of a second chance is everyone's choice. A person will or they won't. Thinking about something will not accomplish anything. Be like R. Buckminster Fuller, the creator of the geodesic dome, be a VERB, be an action word. Second chances are squandered every day by almost everyone. Take time to touch another living soul and burn a hole in the universe with your passion and purpose for life.

9

What is a Cardiac Arrest
and How Do You Prevent It?

That day, January 23, 2006, on the airplane, I experienced a myocardial infarction or a heart attack. My heart attack symptoms came suddenly. I experience what some people describe as a silent heart attack. There were probably warning signs that I did not pay full attention to prior to my event. Looking back, I had some mild discomfort in my chest that I attributed to chest muscle pain. I did feel pressure in my chest but it was not too uncomfortable. It was later explained to me that a piece of plaque broke off and lodged in my main coronary artery, the aorta. This caused a blockage that generated the heart attack. The rhythm of my heart was disrupted, went into fibrillation and it chose to stop beating. I was dead within minutes.

Could it have been prevented? I don't know. I think I did everything right. Perhaps if I had gone in for a stress test within the previous few months, they might have picked up the potential for blockage and a heart attack. I did take a stress test about two years earlier, though, and was given a clean bill of health. Looking back, I did receive a warning one year earlier from my family physician to watch my blood sugars and cholesterol more closely. You know, I think most people would rather deny the seriousness of anything that could go wrong. I was unwilling to accept that I might have to change the way I was eating and living. I wanted to believe that I had no family history of heart disease and that I was immune.

I think the first step in preventing a heart attack that could lead to a cardiac arrest is to listen. Pay attention to your physician, and listen to the rhythm of your body. Your body is telling you things every day and a choice is often made to ignore it. Pay attention to potential warning signs and work on the basics of prevention.

Prevention can be gained by reading and becoming familiar with medical information relating to heart disease. There is a wealth of knowledge out there that will explain the risks and the warning signs of heart disease. Too often, we blunder through life with sound bites, a little bit of knowledge and a whole lot of misinformation that we have picked up here and there.

I know several people who experienced some symptoms that looked like a heart attack. They went in and it was later determined that they had a severe case of indigestion or it was blamed on stress. Embarrassed and put out by their over reaction these people have put themselves at risk later by ignoring other signs of a heart attack when they did occur. When it comes to your heart, do not worry about over-reacting. Not taking action is what causes death. Now is the time to look at what you can do to prevent that heart attack.

The American Heart Association is a great resource for information on heart health and signs of a heart attack. Your family physician will have more information on the subject as well.

Some general signs of a heart attack are:

You feel a tightness or pressure in your chest. You feel heavy pain in your chest. You feel a pain that extents from your chest into the jaw or shoulder. Generally pain is the left shoulder or arm, in my case, I had pain in my right shoulder and arm. In women the signs may be more subtle the pain may be in the jaw and chest. You just cannot seem to catch your breath. Sometimes a heart attack may seem like severe heartburn. You cannot ignore the signs, get help immediately. Get yourself checked out right then. The longer you delay the greater chance you will experience more severe heart damage.

When it comes to heart attack prevention take a serious look at lifestyle choices. Lifestyle choices like, the ones I describe in the prior chapters; eating every meal healthier, an aggressive exercise regimen, not smoking, restricted use of alcohol and getting a good night's sleep in all likelihood could, naturally, turn around your trend towards heart disease and the potential for a cardiac arrest.

Managing stress is another factor to lowering the risk of a heart attack. I have read that some stress is actually good and your body kind of feeds on it in order to keep you competitive and alert. Stress is like anything else, take everything in moderation and you will probably do just fine. If you feel that your job, home life or social life is too stressful, a person should set some new goals and find a way to reduce that stress. Identify the exact cause of your stress then work out some inhibitors or a way to circumnavigate the source of the stress. This could be the key to a happier and longer life.

The doctors who treated me told me that Sudden Cardiac Arrest is really an interruption of the rhythm of your heart. This is a disorder called an arrhythmia. The human body is like a great power plant that is constantly generating and discharging electrical charges. The heart has an electrical system that creates or triggers the heartbeat. These electrical signals cause the heart to contract in a normal, rhythmic way. This squeezing of the heart muscle causes blood to be pumped in and out of it. When the signal is interrupted in some way, the pumping action can become rapid and irregular. This irregular action is called ventricular fibrillation. The chambers of the heart are called ventricles and the fibrillation is the quick electronic pulsing of the heart.

When ventricular fibrillation occurs, the lower chambers of the heart begin to fibrillate, or quiver, instead of normally contracting. When that happens, the heart can no longer pump blood. When there is an interruption of blood flow through the body, the brain becomes starved for oxygen and the victim loses consciousness within seconds. Unless an emergency shock is delivered to the heart within minutes to restore rhythm with a defibrillator, death can occur. The EMT's have told me that more than 70% of ventricular fibrillation victims die before reaching the hospital.

Not all cardiac arrests are caused by a heart attack. An interruption in this rhythm can happen to people of any age, at any time. An arrhythmia is a disruption in electrical impulses that causes the heart to pump blood. An arrhythmia can happen in a healthy heart with no consequence, or it can cause a stroke, heart attack, or cardiac arrest and death.

As a Sudden Cardiac Arrest (SCA) survivor, I have had the fortunate opportunity to meet with many SCA survivors. Not all of them were victims of heart disease. Some of them had arrhythmia conditions where the heart simply stopped functioning normally and fibrillated. In one case, an SCA survivor's heart stopped as a result of a dramatic blow to his chest, the result of a car accident. It took several shocks to bring him back.

Some people have a condition known as a heart murmur and live with it for many years when suddenly the heart will begin to fibrillate. Athletes who collapse on the football field have been diagnosed with fibrillation before their heart arrested. These are all young people who seem to be the picture of health, yet they fall victim to this condition. Fighters who get punched in the chest can have a fibrillation from the shock of the impact. None of these people have degenerative heart disease, yet they suffer a cardiac arrest.

A seventeen-year-old young man named Mike from Connecticut had a Sudden Cardiac Arrest while playing at basketball camp. He said he was sitting at the bench when, suddenly he just slumped to his knees. Mikes heart had gone into fibrillation. The camp directors called 911. The first responder arrived from next door and began CPR. An EMT team showed up and applied a shock from an AED. Mike was rushed to the local hospital and then onto a better equipped hospital. Because of the delay before receiving an AED shock, there was some worry that Mike would have brain damage. Mike was unconscious for three days he received treatment at the hospital, Mike began to improve. Mike has a heart condition known as Hypertrophic Cardiomyopathy. This is a genetically related heart condition where the heart walls are thicker than normal and do not allow for adequate ejection of blood from the ventricle. An ICD was implanted in Mikes' chest. He lives today with this devise to shock him when his heart falls into an irregular rhythm.

It is absolutely imperative that all children have a complete and thorough physical checkup before participating in strenuous physical sports. The schools require it, but parents can be too easy-going when it comes to the wishes of their offspring. If there is any concern of an irregular heartbeat, please follow the directions of your family physician. Don't assume it will not happen to your child or to you.

I was fortunate to meet Lisa Salberg during a medical conference at the University of Kansas Hospital. She is a victim of Hypertropic Cardiomyopathy. She tells me that many people can live very long lives and never even be aware of the condition. Most become aware of it when they are young and active. There is a need for more public awareness of this condition so it can be detected and properly diagnosed in more young people before they too collapse with a cardiac arrest.

An echocardiogram can be performed to determine the risk for a cardiac arrest. This is very much like the echo scan that is used on pregnant women to view the fetus. It is a look at the heart in various sectors at one time. It does not look at clogged arteries. The doctor may also measure the ejection fraction or the amount of blood that is ejected out of the ventricles in the heart through a nuclear stress test.

An electrocardiogram (EKG) is another common test that can be performed. This is when they attach all of the electrodes to your body to monitor heart rhythms. This test will pick up the arrhythmia I mentioned earlier. There is also a Holter monitor that is worn on a strap that surrounds the chest. It is a small device that is worn for two days to check and record the heart rhythm. There is also an event recorder that is a small device the size of an MP3 player. This works like the Holter monitor but is turned on by the patient when they feel their heart beating too fast.

Finally, an Electro-physiology study (EPS) allows a catheter or flexible wire to be inserted and then gently moved toward the heart in order to record the electrical signals. Some even have cameras on them so any blockage can be detected along the way. This is the only thorough test that will pinpoint areas in the heart that may be in serious trouble. This is a pretty useful tool because prior heart attacks can be detected with this test as well.

Today there are tests that can be taken to detect genetically related heart conditions. Genetic markers can be detected with these tests that can help doctors take a more targeted approach to treatment. The PGX Health Company has Familion tests that detect mutations that cause cardiac channelopathies. These are rare and deadly heart conditions. Long QT Syndrome (LQTS),

Brugrada Syndrome (BrS) and Catecholaminegric Polymorphic Ventricular Tachycardia (CPVT) are three such conditions.

Testing in families who have genetically related heart conditions can lead to a reduction of Sudden Cardiac Death in their children. SIDS or Sudden Infant Death Syndrome may be averted with early detection and treatment.

How to prevent Sudden Cardiac Death

The difference between Sudden Cardiac Arrest and Sudden Cardiac Death is that when a person suffers a Sudden Cardiac Death, that person simply didn't survive a Sudden Cardiac Arrest. Sudden Cardiac Death is the number one killer in the United States today. It surpasses AIDS, lung cancer, and breast cancer death totals, combined. It is estimated that 400,000 people die in the United States each year of Sudden Cardiac Death. Of those who have a Sudden Cardiac Arrest roughly 88% do not survive. Of the 12% who do survive the Arrest, 50% of those die because of the time and distance it takes to arrive where the patients are able to receive sustained health care.

Sudden Cardiac Death from an abnormal heart rhythm may occur for several reasons. The most common is the build up of plaque and fatty build-ups in the arteries. A prior heart attack can often lead to further heart attacks. In as may as two thirds of Sudden Cardiac Death victims this is the case. A rapid release of adrenaline into the blood through strenuous athletic exercise may also trigger fibrillation. Finally, illegal drug abuse can easily cause the heart to go into a rapid fibrillation and subsequent death for the victim.

I experienced death for about five minutes of time. My heart and brain had stopped functioning. Quick action on the part of the airplane passengers to perform CPR immediately is what prevented me from experiencing permanent brain damage and additional loss of my heart muscle. Four to six minutes is about all you get then you need to have the heart beat restored through defibrillation. The numbers are astounding–the chances of survival are reduced by 7% to 10% with every minute that passes without CPR and defibrillation with an AED. Very few attempts at resuscitation will work after ten minutes.

In every case where there is a Sudden Cardiac Arrest survivor, someone intervened. There was someone to call 911, someone to perform CPR, and someone to use an AED or an in-hospital defibrillator. As many as 40% of all Sudden Cardiac Deaths occur without witness. It's estimated that only 20% of patients who have out-of-hospital cardiac arrest survive long enough to make it to the hospital, be treated and discharged.

The chain of survival are the steps to save a life. The chain includes: early access or intervention by another person, applying CPR, early defibrillation with and AED and rapid response time to an urgent care facility. In my case, all of the links in the chain were working.

It sounds easy enough, just call 911 when someone collapses or falls to the ground unconscious. Yet, people panic, they stand around and feel hopeless. Someone must take action. Do not assume that this is not an emergency situation. Do not assume that the person has just fainted. Begin by asking the victim if they are all right? Shout if you must but try to get a response. Check their neck for a pulse. Look for a medical bracelet or a Red Cross card in their wallet. Try to find out the name of the patient. Then either you dial 911 or get someone else to dial. If you are no where near a phone, send someone. If you are alone, you must begin CPR immediately.

Response by a trained emergency responder may mean the difference between life and death. They will be more likely to have an AED, if one is needed. When the 911 dispatcher gets on the phone, provide as much information as you can. Tell them your situation, your location and any information you can about the victim. Be prepared to do what ever they ask you to do.

CPR: Conventional Cardiopulmonary Resuscitation is a way to pump oxygen still stored in the body through out the body by applying pressure directly over the heart. This is done by coupling your hands together with your arms straight and applying a count of thirty compressions to the middle of the chest. The action should be deliberate up and down motions. Before you begin, slightly tilt the head back so that the victim's airways are clear to take in air. After each thirty compressions, hold the patients nose, (unless it is a small child) and blow air from your mouth directly into the mouth of the victim. You should be able to see the patient's chest rise and fall with this action. Remember, this link in the chain of survival is buying time for the victim until emergency responders can arrive.

The Call and Pump method is a way to perform CPR immediately with little or no training. Training is available from the American Heart Association or the American Red Cross. They will help you find someone who will train you. Another method is to call 1-877-AHA-4CPR or go to www.cpraytime.org. They have a kit that is a twenty-two minute learning tool for family and friends. The kits come with a blow-up CPR mannequin, a CPR skills practice DVD and a resource booklet. I bought one for my family and the cost was around $30. It is money well spent. When I perform speeches on Heart Health, I often bring a kit along to show to the public. CPR is the one skill that every single human being in the country should know how to perform. Just about anyone of any age can perform this life saving skill when the emergency arises.

Early Defibrillation: An Automatic External Defibrillator (AED) is a device that is used to deliver an electronic shock to the heart. This shock is what stops the fibrillating or quivering action and brings it back into a rhythm tic heart beat. The machine will look for a heart beat. If there is one, no shock will be delivered. If there is none, you will be directed by the AED to stand back and a jolt will be given to the victim. After the first shock the machine will check for a heart beat, and then deliver a second jolt if needed. If that does not work, the AED will instruct the user to begin CPR again and then you will go through a cycle where the AED will advise you to stand clear again to deliver another shock.

Anyone can learn to use an AED. Companies that sell them will train people how to use them. The instructions are also printed on the inside of the device's case. Once the leads are attached, most machines will begin to monitor heart rhythm, heart rate, and blood pressure. You may have to use a razor that is included to shave chest hair so the leads will attach properly to the victim.

The only thing that needs to be done is to push the button. This is the action that will deliver the electrical shock to the heart. Most AED's are relatively foolproof.

Nearly anyone of any age can be defibrillated. Guidelines generally include adults and children over fifty-five pounds or eight years of age. Infants can be defibrillated if special pads are used to protect the child.

The AED may not always resuscitate someone in cardiac arrest. If the heart does not respond to electric currents, the AED may not be successful. The heart may have greater damage beyond defibrillation of the heart muscle. Also, I cannot over stress the importance of CPR. Without it, there is far less chance of resuscitation the longer the patient was in ventricular fibrillation. There is only a short window of a few minutes to save a life. AEDs restart the heart, and CPR will push blood and oxygen through to the brain. Both are critical.

Every person who has had a Sudden Cardiac Arrest has died. The use of an AED is a Sudden Cardiac Arrest victim's only chance for recovery and survival. AED's have numerous built-in safeguards and are designed to deliver a shock only if the AED detects fibrillation. So, don't worry about hurting the victim. Don't hesitate to push the button. Most AED's are self-grounded. This means that they can be used in wet conditions and on metal surfaces safely. You are the facilitator for returning that person to the world of the living. Don't be concerned about being at risk for a lawsuit. Remember, that person is already dead, you cannot hurt them you can only save their life with your action. In 2000, President Bill Clinton signed the Cardiac Arrest Survival Act (CASA). CASA provides Federal protection against liability for people who perform Samaritan Acts. If you have specific questions concerning the Good Samaritan Laws in your state, go to www.momsteam.com and look up your state. All fifty states have now passed Good Samaritan laws and many continue to expand the parameters of civil immunity in the hope of encouraging the deployment of more AEDs into the community.

On TV, you see the doctors and nurses yell "Code Blue" and shout "Clear!" before they dramatically jump off the floor and onto the chest of a victim to pound on their chest. That is definitely one for the "don't do this at home" book. In-hospital defibrillators are manual machines and are much larger. They also monitor heart rhythms like the AED's. In hospitals and on TV, the shock is delivered manually by medical personnel who are trained to make that decision. These machines can also perform many other tasks required by in-hospital professionals.

Rapid Response: Rapid Response is a critical step in the chain of survival. On the average, it takes an ambulance or an EMT up to twelve minutes to arrive on an emergency scene in the United States. This average takes into account rural response times as well as high population density areas as well. Survival rates are the highest for victims who receive a defibrillation within the first three to five minutes after collapse. For this to happen, an AED should be onsite anywhere groups of people collect themselves. Sadly, about 95% of all Sudden Cardiac Arrest victims die with CPR alone. Survival rates go up as high as much as 70% when an AED is available and used. That is why it is important to talk to everyone you know to place an AED in a public place

EMT's tell me that between 30% and 50% of all Sudden Cardiac Arrest victims who have been resuscitated die because of the time it takes to get to the hospital. Rapid Response includes all trained medical professionals who can provide advanced care for the ventricular fibrillation of the heart. Rapid Response begins with the emergency medical technicians who will begin to monitor the patient's progress and transmit this data to the receiving hospital. Rapid Response can also include the well-equipped men and women who staff the Medivac services on helicopters. The emergency room physicians and staff review the exact nature of the medical emergency with efficiency and speed and are all important members of this final and critical link in the Chain of Survival for the Sudden Cardiac Arrest patient. The on-staff cardio physiologist and his or her assessment of the patient's symptoms will determine the specific treatment they will receive.

The quicker hospitals get the patient, the better the odds for the outcome. In my case, the pilot on my airplane contacted air traffic control officials in Minneapolis, and they cleared the runway. The pilot tilted the plane on its wing and turned it around for a quick descent into Lindbergh terminal at Minneapolis International Airport. Once the plane hit the ground and rolled to a stop the doors were thrown open within minutes. I was told that from the time the EMTs arrived on the plane to the time a stent was placed in my heart, the total elapsed time was forty-three minutes. Even with the time on the airplane prior to landing, the total elapsed time was a total victory for a Rapid Response program. I have permanent damage to 12% of my heart. This means that I have 88% of my heart left, it could have been much worse. Virtually everything went right, like clockwork. Had there been any delays along the way, I would have suffered even greater heart damage and might not have survived at all. Dr. Lawler, the Cardiologist who treated me at Abbott Northwestern Hospital in Minneapolis, told me, "The people on the plane saved your life. We, at Abbott, saved your heart." Like they say, timing is everything.

10

Call and Pump

If you were asked, "What is the most important thing you could do with your life today?" what would you say? Would it be world peace? Tell a loved one that you love them? Close that important contract? Ask for forgiveness for some wrong? For some people, it is just remembering to take the trash out.

What if I told you that the most important thing you could do with your life today would be to prepare yourself to save another life? Would that be worth your time? Would it be worth five minutes of your life? That is precisely what I am asking you, as a reader of this book, to do.

Anne Peterson of Anne Peterson Productions in the Kansas City area has devoted a significant portion of her life to helping others. She works with governments and public agencies to bring awareness of the critical need to recognize a person who is suffering a Sudden Cardiac Arrest and to take action. Anne has produced several video programs and DVD's for Sudden Cardiac Arrest and CPR Training. She has worked with the Drs. Ewy and Kern of the Sarver Heart Center in Tucson, AZ to bring awareness of Call and Pump to the public.

Call and Pump is a quick and simple method for anyone to remember in a crisis health situation. When you see someone collapse, immediately call 911 for help. Then begin rapid compressions of the chest to keep the blood moving through out the circulatory system until help arrives. Call and Pump simply states that the compressions are enough. Do not take the time to clear blockage or breathe into the victims' mouth, just begin compressions. It will work.

Anne Peterson has produced a training video that does not take long to play. Watch it twice if you have to. Go to www.callandpump.com and click the training video. Share this website with people you know. Encourage everyone you come into contact with to become trained in rapid heart chest compressions.

Practice what you learn so that when that time comes, you will be fully prepared and willing to take the action for saving a life.

You may be thinking, "I could never do that." Believe me, if it were your child, your spouse, or even your pet you would not think twice. Apply that compassion to all human beings and you will be serving your purpose here on earth.

As I stated in previous chapters, when someone collapses, you may not always know the cause of their condition. It is important, however, that you take some kind of action. The use of CPR may not revive that person, but you will be assisting in the all-important task of helping that person's heart pump blood to the organs until help can arrive. In the case of a Sudden Cardiac Arrest, only a shock from an Automatic External Defibrillator (AED) will help to restore rhythm to that person's heart. Even that may not work, but you do not know that. Your goal must be to keep that person's heart pumping oxygen-rich blood to the organs until help is on the scene.

Because some people have a fear or even a personal revulsion to the "mouth to mouth" portion of standard CPR, the "Call and Pump" method was developed. Keep in mind that your goal is to call for help first. Get someone on the phone, call 911, yell for help, or send someone else to get help. Second, your mission is to circulate blood as effectively as possible through the body. "Call and Pump" will require that you pump at a more steady and sustained rate than with the traditional CPR method. Since you will not be breathing air into the passageway of the victim, you will pump and keep pumping until medical help shows up. It is often suggested that your pumping pace should be kept to the Bee Gee's '80's disco hit "Staying Alive." You know, "Ah, ah, ah, ah staying alive, staying alive." That beat will save a life.

Now that you have that tune etched into your mind for the next hour or so, go ahead and play the DVD. I think you will find it worthwhile to watch. Share it with your family and friends and help everyone you know to become a lifesaver. Do your part, for you never know if the life you save might save your own someday.

11

What Can Be Done in the Community?

Don't let anyone kid you, recovering from a heart attack or a Sudden Cardiac Arrest is a full time job. Your first priority is to establish an active game plan for a balance of health, happiness, and spirituality. Once you have made your lists and organized your thoughts and put a plan into place, it would be a good thing to make the most of your second chance and look at what you can do for others.

If you devote a part of your life to helping others, even in a small way, I believe you will heal faster. There really is something to giving of yourself. My grandmother used to say, "If you are working on someone else's problems you don't have time to worry about your own." She also used to say, "if my string were in a knot, patience would untie it." It was wisdom like hers that confused me as a child. Now that I am an adult, I do my best to confuse my own grandchildren with homilies and metaphors. In my own small way, I am helping them to understand the meaning of life.

I encourage you to do what you can to help others. What you do is up to you. You may work on a Habitat for Humanity project or spend time reading to seniors at a retirement home. The first thing to do is to start with what you know. Focus on what you know about yourself and what knowledge you can share. I know a senior who is retired and decided to become a clown with the Shriners at Children's Hospitals. He said, "You are never too old to be a clown." They sound like words to live by to me. He had cancer and, in many ways, it helped him through his condition.

If you want to help other people, the first thing you must understand is that you are unique. Each of us is endowed with a special talent or skill. What good is that skill or talent that we possess if we do not share it? Believe me, you won't take it with you, so it does no good to hide your skills.

Some people are already active in their church or civic organizations. If you are one of those people, you are way ahead of most folks. You may or may not be active but if you have had a Sudden Cardiac Arrest you are now twice unique. You are once unique for being yourself, and again unique for having died and returned to life. You should seek out others who have also had this experience. Make room in your life to share your experience with another survivor and listen to their experience. Work with other survivors and their families to help save lives. Seek out those who have had heart attacks and share your stories with them. Let them know that there is a reason to make changes in their lives. Work to encourage approval of legislation for the funding of Automatic External Defibrillators (AED's) in public places. Work for public education and training for CPR and help bring attention to the fact that children are dying each year from genetically related heart conditions that can be tested for and easily treated with and ICD.

Seek out a local Sudden Cardiac Arrest Survivor organization. You do not need to have gone through the death experience to be in that organization. If there is not one in your community, help to organize one. Go to meetings and help organize events where others who have had a Sudden Cardiac Arrest can come and would feel comfortable sharing their experiences. Only by bonding together, will we be able to increase the survival rate of Sudden Cardiac Death which currently is between 5% to 7% nationally. Why can't the survival rate be increased to 15% or even 30% in the United States? It can, if everyone who reads this book works to help place AEDs in as many places as possible. Roughly (because the actual number is unknown), 40,000 lives saved, is just six more percent. That could be a loved one, a friend, a co-worker, a celebrity, a stranger. The life you save could be your own.

If you have had a heart attack, the next Sudden Cardiac Arrest victim really could be you. That is why you should get involved. Age does not make a difference, young or old we are all in this together.

What is the value of a human life? This rhetorical question has been asked over and over again for years. The cost could be just a few minutes of your time, a dollar, a hundred dollars, or even ten-thousand dollars. If you lose someone you love, it would be worth any dollar amount to have him or her back with you. The cost of one AED is between $900 and $2,500. The use of that AED in a life saving situation is priceless.

Finding a local Sudden Cardiac Arrest group is not that hard. Log on to the Sudden Cardiac Arrest Association website at www. suddencardiacarrest.org. Awareness of Sudden Cardiac Death is just emerging. There may not be an organization near you. Be patient, contact the SCAA through their website. They may have contacts in your area that can help you find other people who have had a Sudden Cardiac Arrest. It may just be up to you to get a program going in your community. The people at SCAA can help you get started.

Even if you are not a member of a local Sudden Cardiac Arrest group you can get started anytime. In fact, now is a good time to contact everyone you can think of to help place AED's in public places. If the people you know are elected, it might be a good time to remind them that they are, in fact, elected and may come up for another election sometime soon. People such as:

- US Senator

- US Congressperson

- State Senator

- State Assemblyperson

- County Commission

- Mayor/Alderman

- School Board official

- Union/Employee Organization

- People at church

- People where you work

- Where ever you shop, trade or do business, let everyone know they should have an AED on hand

- People who own restaurants, movie theaters, car dealerships and department stores

Sometimes the loudest sound can be a whisper. You can be a very powerful voice by just exercising your interest in something. You do not need money or influence to begin, all you need is the desire to make yourself heard. You may do this through public awareness as another way to get the word out about the need to save more lives from Sudden Cardiac Death. A few things that you can do on your own are:

- Conduct local neighborhood CPR parties and discuss the need for a neighborhood AED. You could always offer Tupperware® as the door prize.

- Conduct neighborhood CPR training. The local Red Cross will help you here. Invite the local press. They might be looking for a human-interest story for a slow news day.

- Get local businesses to put a message in their direct mail pieces as a public awareness campaign. I don't think you will find too many CPR and AED notices posted to pizza boxes, but there is always hope.

- Post the need and the statistics of Sudden Cardiac Death in church bulletins, company newsletters, and club notices. That ought to send a message—especially around personnel review time.

- Contact the PTA and local recreational league youth sporting organizations and stress the need to have an AED at event. Stress the need to have an AED placed in every school and train every child how to perform rapid compression CPR.

- Just make up some homemade handbills and flyers and hand them out at public events and festivals. Let people know the statistics and how to prevent death.

- Begin an e-mail blitz to everyone you know.

- Set-up booths to promote the use of AED's and CPR training at all public events. I wouldn't recommend a public demonstration unless you are using one of the "CPR Anytime" or "AED Anytime" kits that you can obtain through the American Heart Association.

- Contact the American Heart Association. Ask how and where you can help.

- Make sure that every marathon and bicycle race has an AED on hand. Remember, Jim Fixx died of a Sudden Cardiac Arrest right after completing a marathon.

- Print a T-shirt with an AED or CPR message. I don't know about sponsoring a girls' youth soccer team with the message on the back of the t-shirts that says, "Sudden Cardiac Arrest," but the thought did occur to me.

- Print up some business cards with AED or CPR messages on them, and hand them to everyone you meet.

- Support the Red Dress Project in your local community. This is a fantastic women's awareness campaign devoted to spreading the word about women's heart health issues and risk for heart disease.

- Contact and support your local Sudden Cardiac Arrest Support group.

- Just tell everyone you know about this book and that together we can actually save lives.

- Visit your doctor and get a check-up. Do not delay if you have not had a complete and thorough physical and blood work-up.

Organizations that work for preventing Sudden Cardiac Death are out there. I have listed a few for you to contact:

Sudden Cardiac Arrest Association:

This is the national organization for Sudden Cardiac Arrest survivors and their families. They will help you organize and form a local chapter of Sudden Cardiac Arrest survivors. The SCAA identifies and unites survivors, those at risk of SCA, family, friends and colleagues of survivors and those who didn't survive, as well as emergency response providers and medical professionals.

If you have survived a Sudden Cardiac Arrest (SCA), you should contact the Sudden Cardiac Arrest Association (SCAA) and let them know that you are a survivor or that you have a family member who is a survivor. Post your survival story at their website and ask them what you can do.

The SCAA can use your help. They promote an increased awareness of SCA issues, immediate bystander action, public access to defibrillation and therapies through a website and a speaker's bureau. They can also provide materials for information about SCA. The SCAA will also develop and help you grow grassroots membership to advance public policy changes at national, state and local levels. They are advocates for change and co-lead the SCA Coalition to advocate federal legislative policies regarding SCA awareness and legislation.

"The Sudden Cardiac Arrest Association's mission is to prevent loss of life from Sudden Cardiac Arrest. We seek to increase awareness, encourage training for immediate bystander action, increase public access to defibrillation and promote the use of available medical devices and therapies, principally, implantable cardioverter defibrillators (ICD). SCAA members are the beneficiaries of improved science and medical technology, coupled with the wisdom and caring of thousands of physicians."

You can find more information concerning the SCAA at www.suddencariacarrest.org. A blog and community communication tool can be found at http://cardiacarrest.clinicahelth.com.

Sudden Cardiac Arrest Foundation

"The mission of the Sudden Cardiac Arrest (SCA) Foundation is to prevent death and disability from Sudden Cardiac Arrest. The vision of the SCA Foundation is to increase awareness about Sudden Cardiac Arrest and influence attitudinal and behavioral changes that will reduce mortality and morbidity from SCA. Specifically, we envision that our efforts will help:

- Increase the rate of bystander CPR from 20% to 30% within five years;

- Double the use of AED's outside the hospital within five years (increase from 5% to 10%);

- Double the rate of survival to hospital discharge within ten years (increase from 7% to 14%)."

The SCA Foundation can be found at www.scaaware.org. They are an organization devoted to sharing information concerning Sudden Cardiac Arrest and uniting survivors.

Local Chapters of Sudden Cardiac Arrest Survivors Support Groups

My event took place on an airplane over Minnesota and because I was taken to a hospital in Minnesota, I became a member of the Minnesota Sudden Cardiac Arrest Survivors Network. This is a collection of several clubs and organizations through out Minnesota and Iowa. I also started an organization in the Kansas City area, (Heart of America Sudden Cardiac Arrest Survivors Network) www.hoascasurvivor.org that is affiliated with the Minnesota organizations and the SCAA. I can thank the Minnesota SCA Survivors Network for the breakthrough in my healing process. The survivors and their families have become a second family to me and they never fail to remind me of my second birthday each year. Second birthdays are those that celebrate the rebirth of a survivor after a Sudden Cardiac Arrest.

The American Heart Association

www.americanheart.org

Their mission is "to reduce disability and death from cardio-vascular diseases and stroke. That single purpose drives all we do. The need for our work is beyond question." Take the time to contact this worthwhile organization, ask questions, and see where you might fit in.

Red Dress and Go Red for Women

www.goredforwomen.com

"Go Red for Women began in February 2004 to raise awareness that heart disease is women's number one killer. The grassroots campaign has since grown into a vibrant national movement as more women, men, celebrities, healthcare providers and politicians embrace and elevate the cause of women and heart disease."

"The campaign provides women tips and information on healthy eating, exercise, and risk factor reduction, such as smoking cessation, weight maintenance, blood pressure control and blood cholesterol management." The following was taken from the Go Red for Women's Web page. It details the many activities that you can get involved with:

- **Go Red For Women Day**[SM] A national observance created by the American Heart Association, on February 4, thousands of people, including employees at more than 3,000 companies, national and local news anchors and talk-show hosts will wear red to support the cause. The red dress and the color red are symbols for women and heart disease and the American Heart Association's **Go Red for Women** movement.

- **National landmarks and monuments.** National and local landmarks—including the Seattle Space Needle, Niagara Falls, the Empire State Building, Graceland and more—will be illuminated in red during February, American Heart Month to further raise awareness of women and heart disease.

- **The Red Dress Pin—Get One. Give One.** Thousands have already added the red dress pin to their fashion accessory collection to support the women and heart disease movement. This year, women are urged to get two free red dress pins—one to wear and one to share with someone they care about. You can get the pins by calling 1-888-MY-HEART.

- **National Celebrity Spokesperson.** Grammy award-winning R&B vocalist Toni Braxton, among several celebrities involved in **Go Red for Women,** is the national spokes-woman in 2005. "I am so pleased to be joining **Go Red for Women**, not only because heart disease has touched me personally, but also because I can assist in taking the message to the thousands of women who don't know that heart disease is their number one health risk," she said.

- **Red Dress Statue Collection.** More than twenty celebrities in fashion, music, food, television, film, and sports have inspired a unique collection of custom-designed statues depicting the **Go Red for Women** red dress icon. The statues will be unveiled on February 3, at Radio City Music Hall. The celebrities include Bill Cosby, Antonio Banderas, Melanie Griffith, Jamie Lee Curtis, Daisy Fuentes, Jane Pauley, Univision TV personality Teresa Rodriguez, designers Carolina Herrera, and TV chefs Rachel Ray and Sara Moulton.

- **Shop with Heart at ShopGoRed.org.** This February, with the launch of the Go Red for Women Online Store, consumers can get important health information as well as shop for fun products that benefit the American Heart Association. The site offers a brand new rhinestone red dress pin as well as hats, bags, scarves and even a men's tie. The site is the only source of official **Go Red for Women** merchandise from the American Heart Association.

- **Shop for A Great Cause.** There are many products "benefiting" the American Heart Association from Day-Timers, Le Mystere lingerie, Perfumania, Brighton, Swarovski Crystal, and more. These products, on sale through February and beyond (in some cases), are also linked to at **ShopGoRed.com**.

- **The scientific community joins the movement.** At a news conference on February 1, the American Heart Association will release new scientific statements on women and heart disease as well as a new study on what physicians and consumers are doing (or not doing) to reduce their risks.

Anyone can join Go Red for Women by calling 1-888-MY-HEART (1-888-694-3278) or visiting www.americanheart.org.

The subject of Men's Heart Health

I decided to approach the subject of men's health separately. Statistically, we know that men are more likely than women to have a heart attack and Sudden Cardiac Arrest. Men, however, are less likely to talk with other men—or anyone for that matter—about themselves, especially with regard to their health issues.

I was speaking with a woman the other day who had lost her younger brother, a man in his 40's to a heart attack. It is suspected that he had a Sudden Cardiac Arrest and died. There was no one around when he experienced his event. She said that she found out later from his friends that he was experiencing many of the warning signs of a heart attack. He said that he had lots of gas that caused chest pain. He would occasionally complain of pain in his arms and shoulders. He felt tired and had a shortness of breath now and then. He did not seek medical help and he died. Her brother is not unlike a lot of men. Men tend to ignore heart problems or disregard them. They probably realize what is going on, they just do not want to deal with the issue or they deny it exists.

What we should do (and, most often, don't) is to encourage men to get checkups and take steps to get healthy. Men need to feel comfortable talking to other men about this. I know it is more fun to talk about the sports scores or your golf game but bring up the subject. Get the PSA (Prostate Specific Antigen), blood glucose, homocysteine, triglycerides, cholesterol, a urinalysis, colon, and colonoscopy check-ups.

Just do it is an advertising slogan that makes sense for hearth health. What you do not know can—and will—hurt you. Putting it off may result in death. My best friend died because he chose not to know about his colon cancer. He ignored the warning signs and when he knew, he blew it off as nothing serious. You can and you will die if a serious condition is ignored. You do not have to die a miserable and hurtful death because you would not check it out.

The reason men need to talk to men is that there is no male specific awareness program that I am aware of. There needs to be a national awareness program for men, too. The little blue pill ads and the promise of three hours of fun are all we get. Believe it or not, your heart is a much more important organ. The Red Dress program for women is a wonderful example of how to draw attention to a serious problem. Men need some kind of a campaign that works. Perhaps a red TV remote or football might get men to focus on the need to get checked out and take appropriate action for their heart health. My son tells me that Spike TV has some promotions for men's health. I am not sure I know how many people in my demographic watch Spike TV, but it is a start.

I am a spokesperson for Sudden Cardiac Arrest awareness. As such, I have told my story before a variety of audiences and in many venues. The one common theme at each of these presentations is the fact that most people are unaware of the dramatic number of deaths each year from Sudden Cardiac Death. In every venue that I have spoken, someone has advised me that as a result of my speech, they have taken action to obtain an AED or to get CPR training.

As part of my second-chance goals, it's my personal mission to help save the lives of as many people as possible and to stop the senseless death rate. We know the cause, and we know how to stop it. We just need to get the job done. In some small way, your reading this book has helped. Hopefully, you are a little more educated to a major killer in the United States and the world at large. The next step is up to you. What do you need to do to help someone else get a second chance at life?

12

Some Heart Felt Thoughts

A few days ago, I asked my youngest daughter how things were going for her. She told me that she was okay, but not perfect. How true that is for all of us! I said "if things were perfect, what would you have to shoot for?" How would you know if you were making progress? Life is not perfect for me either. I have to pay bills, deal with stress, and, physically, I have my up days and my down days. The drugs still wreak havoc with my body from time to time. Some days I can feel the pressure in my chest, and other days I am just physically drained. Some days I feel like I could run a marathon. I have come to grips with my condition, and I'm learning to live with it. All in all, I'm coping with survival.

My medication regimen continues to change. Some blood sugar medications tend to retain water and increase the risk of heart failure while others will enslave you to a visit to the bathroom on a regular basis. Cholesterol statins are hard on the liver and the effects of blood pressure medicines can literally sweep you off your feet. There is the on-going debate over drug coated stents, whether drugs like Plavix need to be taken indefinitely or not to prevent clotting from occurring. I am not sure if a heart by-pass was ever considered for my particular medical condition but the theory behind a stent seemed to make sense to me.

The author's stent placement

In my case, the physicians on hand agreed that an angioplasty and stent placement would be the best treatment to use. They explained to me, at the time, that there was some risk. I was told that is an operative procedure and death could occur. Having just been through a death experience I thought "what the heck."

They explained quickly, that a stent was like a miniature chain link fence and would be placed into the area where the artery had been constricted with plaque. The stent would literally hold that part of the artery open, allowing the blood to flow freely to the heart.

I had a drug-coated stent placed in my main coronary artery. I was given a card in the hospital with the stent information on it with a picture of a heart and a mark where my clog had been. I carry that card with me, even today.

In a way, I was feeling fortunate as I laid there on the table, having them explain all of this to me. My body was still trying to arrest again and, in the back of my mind, I felt as though they were probably going to perform heart bypass surgery. I was not looking forward to the encounter. I must admit I was somewhat relieved when they explained the angioplasty procedure and the stent placement to me.

The stent has been installed in my body and I am living with it today. There has been a lot published both pro and con on the use of drug-coated stents. My area of expertise is the automotive dealership business, so I will offer no intelligent discourse on a subject out of my field. I was told that I would need to take a drug called Plavix for an unspecified time, perhaps for as long as I live. Except for the fact that it is patent protected and there are no generic replacements, I figure, what the heck, what is one more drug to the long list of medications I am taking daily.

Plavix I am told, is not an extract from the illusive Duck Billed Plavix of southern Australia. It was explained to me as being kind of like "Slick-50 oil" for the blood stream. It coats the insides of the arteries to prevent any further build-up of plaque.

The way it works is that a stent tube is collapsed to a very small diameter and a balloon catheter is inserted into the tube. The catheter is then inserted into the femoral artery in the groin area. This is a pretty sensitive procedure because with one quick move and the artery is pierced and you could bleed to death. Carefully, the catheter is snaked up into the heart area where the aorta resides. In my case it was where the blockage was. The catheter balloon is inflated and the stent is expanded and it locks in place and holds the walls of the aorta open for blood to flow freely.

The main advantage of a stent is that no by-pass surgery was performed. The other main advantage of a stent is that it reduces the re-narrowing of the artery walls after an angioplasty. There is always the possibility that a stented artery can reclose. Clotting can occur or even the re-build up of plaque that will close a stent. That is why drug therapy and a healthy lifestyle are important. They can assist in preventing re-closing of a stent.

I think my stent is doing what it is advertised to do, keep my aorta open so that I get good oxygenated blood through out my body. There is no way to know of course, unless the doctors should decide to re-insert another catheter into my body and take a look.

I continue to work and fly through out the country. I have a medical identification necklace that I wear around my neck that identifies me as a heart patient with diabetes. Only once did I have to take it off for an airport security check. They also took my bottle of nitroglycerin. At one point I thought they were going after the metal stent in my heart but, of course they could not detect that.

I think it is good to get back into a busy life after a trauma such as a Cardiac Arrest. I probably did more than I should have immediately following my event. That is why I struggled with medications and healing issues. I should have paced it better, but that is Monday morning quarterbacking.

As I mentioned diabetes is a dogfight. It is a struggle because at any point in time I can have a radical mood swing and say or do something that would normally be inconceivable to me. Things can seem fine with my sugars running in a normal range, under 130 and then, with out warning, they just shoot up for no apparent reason. My sugar can also take a nosedive and I just seem to visibly sink. It is this yo-yo action that is the most difficult to cope with. Like I said, I am doing all right but I am not perfect.

If I can do one thing with this book it is to simply save lives. I want every heart patient who reads this book to take to heart the lifestyle changes they need to make for reasons that mean something only to them and then make a plan and take action. This could prevent the unnecessary experience of a Sudden Cardiac Arrest.

I want first responders and emergency room personnel and Cardiology professionals to know the human side of a clinical condition known as a Sudden Cardiac Arrest. I want them to know that the healing process begins when the patient gets home. Patients are people who have very real lives that just don't stop for the families and co-workers around them when something like this happens. They need to understand that change is not an easy thing to accomplish. It requires coaching and positive support. Doctors need to impress on their patients the joy of living rather than the drudgery of stop or die. Finally, the medical community needs to become partners with survivors to help improve the survival rate of other Sudden Cardiac Arrest victims in the community.

I want people to read this book to seriously look at what they can do to learn CPR and help place AED's in public places. This action will save lives and improve the miserable 94% fatality record of Sudden Cardiac Death. I want more young children to grow up to be contributing adults, to make music, create poems and build bridges. I want people everywhere around this globe to have the opportunity to savor life sustaining oxygen as it is re-introduced into their blood streams because someone somewhere was thoughtful enough to learn CPR or place an AED for quick access.

It is so important that every loved one, every human being have one more opportunity for a second chance when their time calls for it. I am having my second chance at life, don't you think it is time you helped someone else have their second chance?

13

Survivor's Stories

These are the stories of Sudden Cardiac Arrest victims. The one thing they all share is that they died. In some cases, it took several shocks with an AED to bring them back. Their stories are a marvelous testament for placing more and more AED's into public places. For the most part, the stories are all told in the words of the victim, they way they wanted to explain their event.

Keep in mind that the survival rate in southern Minnesota has gone up over 300% in the last three years mostly to the efforts of many of the survivors in this chapter. They are all heroes and heroines. Like me, they struggle from day to day with their physical disabilities but they persevere and many have devoted a portion of their lives to saving other lives.

Natasha (age 33)

Natasha, who is thirty-three, suffered a Sudden Cardiac Arrest while at work. Her co-workers applied CPR to her and called 911. The EMT's arrived quickly and used a defibrillator to shock her back to life. She was diagnosed with idiopathic dilated cardiomyopathy. She now has an implanted ICD. She is currently active with "Go Red" and the American Heart Association supporting women with heart health issues. She stays physically active and takes long bike rides. She is a mother of two boys, ages seven and ten.

Kelly (age 15)

Kelly is an active teenager, age fifteen. She and a couple of her friends were jumping on a trampoline and shooting hoops. As they returned to the house, Kelly suddenly collapsed. At first, her two friends thought she was just playing around. When she didn't respond to their questions, they realized that she was in serious trouble. The girls didn't panic, and they took immediate action. They called 911 and began to apply CPR. Less than two minutes later, the local police department arrived. The police department had an AED and used it immediately. An ambulance showed up shortly. One of the girls called Kelly's parents and they came immediately. Kelly's father is a Paramedic, and he was able to assist in Kelly's recovery. Kelly was taken to the hospital and she was implanted with an ICD. Today, she lives an active and healthy life, although she must avoid strenuous physical activity. She is now in college and doing well.

Gene (age 63)

Gene is a retired school teacher who was laying sod in his yard. His wife was inside working on household chores when she received a phone call from her daughter. Her daughter, who lives across town, ask what her dad, Gene, was doing. She asked her mother to check on him. Gene's wife went outside immediately and saw him lying on the ground. She then called 911. The paramedic showed up four minutes later. They used an AED that was only one of two units in that town. The paramedic who showed up was one of Gene's former students. Gene was sixty-three at the time of this event. He was shocked back to life and a heartbeat was detected, but Gene did not regain consciousness. He was taken to the hospital where he remained unconscious for thirty-six hours before he received bypass surgery. Today, he is physically active and takes his medication faithfully. His daughter said that Gene had visited her and talked to her while he was unconscious, and that's what prompted her call to her mother that day.

Paul (now age 60)

Paul, who is now sixty, suffered a Sudden Cardiac Arrest while working at an election-polling site. He was shocked once with an AED and taken to a hospital. Later it was determined that he would need triple-bypass surgery. Paul now has an ICD and a pacemaker to help keep his heart in rhythm.

Butch (age 55)

Butch, who is in his fifties, suffered a Sudden Cardiac Arrest while finishing a play onstage. His responders used an AED. He was shocked twenty-two times before his heart became somewhat stable and was taken to the hospital. Butch, who lives in a rural area, has seen both sides because he is also a member of a local volunteer group who assist residents in medical emergencies until an ambulance can arrive. His volunteer group bought an AED and had the opportunity to respond to an emergency. Butch used the defibrillator and saved another man's life. This all happened one year before Butch had his SCA event.

Clayton (age 71)

Clayton, who is in his seventies, had a Sudden Cardiac Arrest while he was shoveling snow in his driveway. A neighbor saw him fall, rushed out, and began performing CPR. A snowplow driver happened to be driving by and stopped to give assistance. He called 911, and a firefighter heard the call. She knew Clayton and rushed to the scene and provided a shock with an AED. Clayton was taken to the hospital where they used five stents to open his arteries. He was implanted with an ICD. His recovery has been complicated with back problems related to back and spinal surgery that he had years before. He also has arthritis and osteoporosis, but Clayton uses a walker and attends cardio rehab weekly.

Mary (age 44)

Mary, who is in her forties, had a Sudden Cardiac Arrest while she was at work. Her co-workers used CPR and an AED that their office had installed the prior year. She was shocked twice and her heart resumed rhythm. She was taken to the hospital. Mary had an arrhythmia that could be reproduced in the hospital so they implanted an ICD. Later, Mary was traveling on a business trip and was in her hotel room, alone. She had a second Sudden Cardiac Arrest and was saved by her implantable Cardio Defibrillator (ICD). Mary is very active in leading the placement of AED's in Iowa and is a spokesperson for early detection of arrhythmia conditions.

Kat (age 54)

Kat is a fifty-four-year-old woman who had a Sudden Cardiac Arrest while her adult daughter and sister watched. The sister began CPR immediately and her daughter called 911. They each provided CPR, and the fire department responded within two minutes. They began use with a ResQPod which is a cardiac support pump that improves circulation for the heart. They also assisted with CPR. The paramedics arrived and used an AED. Kat was shocked eight times before being transported to the hospital. She was prepped and taken to a Cardiac Care Unit where they induced hypothermia protocol (cooled her body temperature). Kat woke immediately following the completion of warming. The following Friday, Kat received an Implantable Cardioverter Defibrillator (ICD). Kat is a spokesperson for her local "Take Heart" program for public awareness. Kat is doing well today.

Gerald (age Mid 40's)

Gerald (Jerry) was umpiring a softball game, when he suddenly suffered a Sudden Cardiac Arrest. A police officer was driving by within three blocks of the ball field when the 911 call came in. He just happened to have a shared AED in his car at the time. He and another officer take turns carrying the device. The other officer was more than three miles away at the time. Jerry was revived with a single shock and was transported to the local hospital, where an ICD was implanted.

Terry (age 56)

Terry, a fifty-six-year-old man who was driving on the freeway when he began to see bright lights. He took the next exit and pulled to a stop in the middle of an intersection. The next thing he knew, an officer was over him and had shocked him back to life with an AED. Terry was still strapped in the driver's seat by his safety belt when he was resuscitated. Terry is very active with the placement of AED's in his community and has worked hard to earn grant money for his local chapter of his cardiac arrest survivors group.

Fran (age mid 20's)

Fran, a young woman, was visiting her daughter's pediatrician when she experienced a Sudden Cardiac Arrest in the stairwell. Her daughter alerted the doctor's office personnel. They responded immediately with a crash cart that had a defibrillator on it. She was revived within minutes. She suffered heart damage (pericardium cardiomyopathy), in spite of the rapid response. She was transported to the hospital where they implanted an ICD. Now, fifteen years later, she is on her third ICD and doing quite well.

Kathy (age 41)

Kathy has a condition known as Hypertrophic Cardiomyopathy. This is an inherited condition where the heart muscle is thicker than it should be. As a result, the heart has a hard time ejecting the blood out of the ventricle and circulating it throughout the body. Sometimes an arrhythmia occurs and the heart goes into fibrillation. This condition is discovered mostly in young people. Kathy was aware of this condition prior to suffering a Sudden Cardiac Arrest at age forty-one. She was shocked four times to recover. Twelve years later, she is living with an ICD and is full of energy.

Teresa (age 12)

At the age of twelve, Teresa was running to second base in a softball game, when she suffered a Sudden Cardiac Arrest. Two nurses and two police officers were at the ball game and applied CPR immediately. The police officers used an AED to revive Teresa. She spent two weeks in a hospital and received an ICD. The ICD has saved her on some other occasions and now, at age twenty-one she is the mother of a four-year-old and a one-year-old. Currently, she feels great and is active in her local Sudden Cardiac Arrest chapter.

Rodney (age 63)

Rodney suffered his Sudden Cardiac Arrest at age sixty-three. A nurse gave him CPR while a doctor who was on site, checked him over. He was shocked back with an AED from the arriving ambulance six minutes after his collapse. He did not sustain any heart damage and does not have an ICD. He is now seventy-seven and has some concern about the future, so his doctor wrote an approval for him to carry an AED with him. He received the AED through Medicare. He was the first in his state to do so.

Don (age 54)

Don, a fifty-four-year-old man, was sitting in a recliner, half watching golf on TV and half dozing asleep. His family was all around him because they were celebrating both Father's day and his anniversary with his wife, Lorie, that day. He suffered a Sudden Cardiac Arrest. His wife, who is a nurse, began CPR while his son called 911. Firefighters and police officers showed up and used an AED to shock him back to life. His doctor inserted an ICD, for peace of mind and it has never gone off. Don is now sixty. He and his wife have now celebrated their fortieth wedding anniversary.

Ray (age 74)

Ray was seventy-four years old when he had his Sudden Cardiac Arrest. He was in the hospital when it happened and was defibrillated there. He was unconscious for six weeks. He spent a total of seventy days in the heart hospital and suffered considerable heart damage. He received an ICD four months after his event. He now walks using a cane. He did have an unusual ICD malfunction where his unit shocked him a total of thirty-six times before they could fix what was setting it off. Ray, like many who have had a Sudden Cardiac Arrest, experienced a very profound after death experience. Ray is very active working to place AED's in sheriff department vehicles throughout his state.

Al (age 40)

In 1994, Al was home resting after complaining of some pain in his chest. He awoke from his rest with symptoms of a heart attack. He was sweating and had chest pain. His son called 911, and an ambulance arrived within minutes. He received a shock from an older model AED that had paddles instead of the leads that are now used. He was transported to the hospital where he received double-bypass surgery. He is now doing fine. Al was forty at the time of his Sudden Cardiac Arrest. He is very active in his SCA support group.

Roger (age mid 70's)

Roger was in his front yard. He had been in his back yard, looking for wood for his fireplace, when he came around to the front and just dropped, right in front of his house. His wife called 911. He was shocked three times by paramedics, and then four times again, and then another four times at the hospital before his heart stabilized. He was implanted with an ICD. He did not have bypass but he did go through cardio rehabilitation. Roger is now eighty years old and getting along well.

David (age 44)

David, who is forty-four, was in his bathroom when he suffered a Sudden Cardiac Arrest. His family heard him fall and began CPR. The local police showed up and did not have an AED. They took over the CPR until the EMT's arrived, some five to six minutes after the 911 call. David was shocked three times before he was revived. David is active and doing great. He, too, works with is local SCA survivor organization to place AED's in public places.

John (age 59)

John was jogging on his treadmill at a fitness center when he had is Sudden Cardiac Arrest. John was fifty-nine at the time. The staff started CPR and dialed 911. They had just installed an AED and they used it to shock John back to life. It took one shock to revive him. He was rushed to the hospital, where they performed triple bypass surgery on his heart. David is back to resuming his normal lifestyle, with plenty of exercise. He recently finished a five-mile race.

Jay (age 51)

Jay suffered a heart attack at fifty-one. Jay actually walked up to the ambulance under his own power. While being transported to the hospital, he went into ventricular fibrillation and had a Sudden Cardiac Arrest. He was shocked back and taken to the hospital. He suffered 50% damage to his heart muscle. He received an ICD. A few months later, he had another relapse and had to call

911 again. This time it was for enlargement of the heart. His ejection fraction will always be 25% to 30%. Jay is active in his SCA support group. He feels the people there understand what it is that he is going through.

Brent (age 43)

Brent, a forty-three-year-old man, suffered his Sudden Cardiac Arrest while he was at home in his bed. He is a pastor in his church. He said that this experience has enriched his faith.

Dick (age 65)

Dick, a sixty-five-year-old man, was attending a wedding reception when he had his Sudden Cardiac Arrest. An EMT happened to be at the reception and began to apply CPR immediately. The local police department showed up with an AED ResQPOD and it took five shocks to revive him. He was taken to the hospital, where they implanted an ICD. He remained unconscious for thirty-six hours and has no recollection, at all, of the event. Dick has had additional surgeries to his legs. Both legs will need new artificial veins and arteries.

Dennis (age 68)

Dennis is a sixty-eight-year-old man who has had a history of heart problems for the last twenty years. He has had a couple of bypass surgeries and uses extensive medication therapy. He has been very active in his local Kiwanis Club. He was with a couple members of that club when he had his Sudden Cardiac Arrest in his home. His friends applied CPR until the paramedics arrived and revived him with an AED. He is feeling relatively well these days and he is very active in his community to raise public awareness of AEDs and the need for more of them.

Wendell (age 62)

Wendell is a sixty-two-year-old man who was shopping at a local grocery store when he had his Sudden Cardiac Arrest. A customer discovered Wendell in the canned food aisle and notified the store manager, who immediately began to apply CPR. The manager had just been trained in CPR just six weeks prior to this event. The police arrived and applied a single shock from an AED. He was taken to the hospital, where they applied hypothermia protocol to cool his body to help save his heart from further damage. They warmed him and he was taken to the cath lab where a stent was placed in his coronary artery. Because of Wendell's Sudden Cardiac Arrest at this particular grocery food chain, they chose to put an AED in every store of their chain.

Arlene (age 65)

Arlene, a sixty-five-year-old woman, was at home with her husband by her side in bed. Her husband said that Arlene visited her in his dream and told him that she loved him and that she would be moving on to another place. He awoke immediately and discovered that she was unconscious. He applied CPR immediately and called 911. The paramedics arrived and she was shocked with an AED to stop the ventricular fibrillation. They used a ResQPOD. She stayed in the hospital for one month where they implanted an ICD. Arlene has very little memory of the entire ordeal.

Lawrence (age 77)

Lawrence is a seventy-seven-year-old man who collapsed in a restaurant bathroom with his Sudden Cardiac Arrest. His wife, who is seventy-three, did not know CPR and there was no trained personnel on hand, so she started the compressions. She had watched a TV program recently where an MD said, "If people would just do chest compressions when someone collapses, then a lot of people would be saved." The restaurant manager traded off with her while she coached him. Paramedics arrived quickly and were able to establish a heart rhythm with four shocks from an AED. Lawrence remained in a coma and was taken to a hospital. He regained consciousness a few days later but was restless, with short-term memory loss. Three days later, he became erratic and paranoid and tore out his IV lines. The next day he awoke alert, calm and oriented. His memory was back, and three days later, he received an ICD and was eventually sent home. Lawrence continues to work and quit smoking.

Dick (age 68)

Dick is a sixty-eight-year-old man who had a history of heart attacks prior to his Sudden Cardiac Arrest. He had his first heart attack in 1995 and experienced some permanent damage to the bottom of his heart. He had a second attack after he had some warning signs. He went to his doctor and told him that he felt uncomfortable, that he might be having a heart attack. The doctor felt that it was probably angina and sent him home to rest. The next day he again felt pains and went to the doctor a second time. This time they called 911 and sent him to the hospital. He was checked in and was given a series of tests, including a stress test. He went into a Code Blue. This is a flat line on the heart monitors. The nurses administered CPR and rubbed his feet and legs. They applied a strong blow to Dick's chest before the defibrillator cart could arrive. His heart began to beat again and ventricular fibrillation was stopped.

Dick told his wife later that while the nurses were working on him that some people came to him, got him up, and escorted him out of the room and took him toward another room. He felt as though they had done it to help him out. He didn't know or recognize any of these people. He said when he got to the other room, they weren't ready to help him and told him that he should go back to his room, so they all went back to where the nurses were. Dick never left his bed. The nurses had continually worked on him until his heart began to beat with a fairly normal rhythm. Dick has had subsequent surgery and still experiences some dull pain from time to time but he is physically active.

Bob (age Mid 30's)

Bob was working at a convenience store gas station during the winter. He was scraping ice away from the gas pumps and decided to go inside to warm up his lunch at the food counter area. He collapsed with a Sudden Cardiac Arrest and the employees called 911. Customers in the store began to apply CPR. The local police department arrived five minutes later and shocked him twice with an AED. The ambulance arrived and Bob was shocked twice again on the way to the hospital. At the hospital they applied a cooling blanket called an "Artic Sun" to lower Bob's body temperature. His temperature was lowered to 92° for twenty-four hours. This was supposed to improve his chances of survival from 5% to 20%. An ICD was implanted a week later.

Chuck (age 60)

Chuck, a sixty-year-old nurse, was entering a local legion club when he collapsed in the doorway with a Sudden Cardiac Arrest. A quick-thinking lady who was standing near him immediately applied CPR. Someone called 911. A local police officer showed up with an AED, and Chuck was shocked back to life. He was taken to a local hospital where he was very unstable. He suffered two more heart attacks before he was stabilized. His ejection fraction is about 20%. Chuck had three leg stents put in and has been put on a list for heart transplant recipients because of the extensive damage to his heart.

Dawn (age 34)

Dawn is a thirty-four-year-old woman who was sleeping on her couch at home. She awoke in her bed with a backache and took some aspirin. She went back to sleep on the couch then awoke again, vomited and then had a Sudden Cardiac Arrest. Her husband is an EMT, and he responded immediately with CPR and called 911. The police department arrived with in four minutes. They brought an AED and shocked her four times to stop the fibrillation and get her heart back to normal rhythm. The fire department arrived, and then had to shock her another five times as they transported her to the hospital. At the hospital, they shocked her multiple times as well. They cooled her body to 90 degrees. She was sent to another hospital, where they implanted two stents and cleared her blockage. She is taking several medications as well as exercising and following diet restrictions to treat her heart condition.

Al (age 64)

Al is a sixty-four-year-old marathon runner. He is a retired police officer and had just finished a twenty-mile run. He couldn't understand why he was so lightheaded and fatigued. He suddenly collapsed with a Sudden Cardiac Arrest on the sidewalk. A woman was standing across the street and saw him drop. A couple was driving by in their car and they stopped, too. They all rushed to his aid. They began to apply CPR immediately and called 911. Within minutes, the local police department showed up with an AED. Al was taken to a local hospital where they inserted a catheter and did an angioplasty and placed a stent in his blocked artery. Al is happy to be alive and is looking forward to running in another marathon.

Benjamin (age 22)

Benjamin is a twenty-year-old who was sleeping at home in his bed. He began breathing oddly. His dog was in another room sleeping with his brother. The dog woke up to Ben's noises and began to bark. The dog's barking woke Ben's brother, who then checked on Ben and discovered that he was in trouble. Ben's brother called his mother—who is a nurse—from the other room and then called 911. His mother began to apply CPR when Ben stopped breathing. Paramedics arrived and shocked Ben six times with an AED before he resumed breathing again. An ICD was implanted at the hospital. He has recovered rapidly and is attending college.

Tammy (age 37)

Tammy is a healthy Mom who is also a nurse. Se was dropping her girls off at soccer practice when she experienced a SCA. She had just lost her father two weeks earlier. Two women came to the van she had been driving when they noticed the engine revving. A physician happened to be passing by and helped to remove Tammy from the van and then began CPR. Paramedics arrived and it took four shocks with an AED to bring her back. She was on a ventilator for three days and in the hospital for seven days. She was implanted with an ICD. She says she has palpitations and arrhythmias from time to time. She is just grateful to be alive. She said that God is not finished with her yet.

Rose Marie (age 60)

Rose was attending a wedding in rural Kansas. She had just stepped to the lectern to perform the reading. As she reached the last sentence, the print blurred and she realized the she could not decipher the words. She then collapsed and fell down a couple of steps. Friends immediately called 911. Other friends rushed to give her CPR. The pastor of the church rushed into another room and grabbed an AED that the church had recently purchased. The leads were attached and it took two shocks to revive Rose. Paramedics arrived quickly and took her to a local hospital. Later she was flown to the Nebraska Heart Institute in Lincoln, NE. No heart blockage was detected. Rose has Long QT Syndrome. She had also taken a decongestant and her potassium was low. She now has an ICD implanted to monitor her heart.

Keith (age 52)

I was an active field hockey coach and I was attending a dinner dance to celebrate the 60th anniversary of our church, when I suddenly collapsed in front of the band. My wife called for help and an off-duty firefighter, was summoned. He performed CPR for about five minutes, together with some nurses who were also at the dinner dance.

One of the church staff members noticed the firefighter performing CPR and asked what was going on. He revealed that I was having a SCA and was awaiting the EMT's. She told him that the church had just received an AED. She brought the AED to shock me to bring me back to life.

After that, the EMT's arrived and took me to the hospital. En route, they told me that I was very lucky to be alive and it was a good thing there was an AED in the building, since it would have been too late for them to save me. I'm very blessed to be alive to tell my story.

Now, I'm a volunteer with the local chapter of the American Heart Association and Project Heart Restart and I give talks about the importance of installing AEDs in all public places.

Tracy (age 38)

Tracy is a stand up comedienne who suffered a Sudden Cardiac Arrest on the set of her comedy show. The show ran for years in the Pacific Northwest before being picked up by cable channel for nationwide broadcasting.

"We were still standing (on the set, after the final skit) and taking questions from the audience when I collapsed," Tracey said in a recent telephone interview.

Volunteer firefighters administered CPR right away and six minutes later, Tracey was given the first of six shocks with an AED. Although Tracey says that she was conscious and talking to friends and relatives after one day, she admits that "I was out of it for four days." Tracy had an ICD implanted.

Tracy has had had numerous invitations to speak about her experience and the part that an AED played in her rescue after her heart stopped on that soundstage as a live studio audience watched in horror.

"I was approached quickly to start telling my story," she said. She decided to become a full-time advocate for the placement of AEDs in all public places while still acting part-time. Now she does about thirty speaking engagements a year for community groups, hospitals and local organizations, and her easy rapport with an audience, her sincerity and her wit has made her a favorite on the American Heart Association's speaking circuit.

From making people laugh to making people aware, Tracey makes a difference.

Sam (age 58)

Sam never realized that he had a flair for the dramatic, but when he suffered Sudden Cardiac Arrest, he did so before a near sellout crowd.

While fans waited for the start of the second half of a high school basketball game, referee Sam came out onto the floor and was waiting for the teams to emerge from their locker rooms when, according to several eyewitness accounts, he hit the floor hard.

"People told me my knees never buckled," said Sam who, like many SCA victims remembers nothing about the event, "I just went straight back."

The fall resulted in eight staples to close the gash in his head, but the more immediate problem was to restore his breathing and heartbeat. Fortunately, two emergency department nurses were in the crowd and they started administering CPR while other fans ran to find a local cardiologist whom they knew was also in attendance.

"They diagnosed me with no breathing and no pulse," Sam said.

Not long before the incident, that same cardiologist had convinced the school to get an AED. After the school's athletic director brought the device to the court, Sam's heart was shocked back into a nice steady rhythm and he was on his way to the hospital.

The diagnosis was sclerosis in one artery, the one that controls the heart's electrical impulse. After angioplasty and the placement of a stent, Sam was sent home with orders to sit out the rest of the basketball season and accept the probability that his refereeing career was over.

"That pissed me off," Sam remembers.

But after a bout of cardiac rehabilitation and some healthy lifestyle choices, the doctor pronounced Sam, who is now entering his 33rd season as both a high school football and basketball official, fit enough to put on the zebra shirt and resume the avocation he loves.

"It hasn't changed me at all," Sam said. "If people hadn't told me it happened to me, I would have believed it happened to someone else."

But, as Sam knows well, it is hard to mistake the real SCA sufferer when the event happens in the presence of so many eyewitnesses.

A Cardiac Arrest can happen anytime, any place. And yes, you too could possibly have one. Do not underrate the symptoms. I met a woman the other day who told me of a pain in her back. When she went in it was determined that she was really having a heart attack. The symptoms may not be what you believe them to be. In my case, the pain was in my right shoulder, not the left. Pain is pain, so be aware of all of the warning signs.

I have placed just a few of the many remarkable stories of people who have all suffered a Sudden Cardiac Arrest. I did not have room for all of them. The one thing that all of these wonderful people have in common is that another person intervened on their behalf. They all suffered a cardiac arrest and all but one of them was all shocked back to life with an AED.

14

Quick Reference Guide to Medical Jargon, Acronyms, and Terms for Heart Patients

Once you have had a cardiac event, you become acutely aware of the language surrounding your condition. Initially, most of the words and phrases used are alien and uncomfortable. The medical community freely uses these terms every day. They are very comfortable using the language with which they communicate with each other. Often, when professional medical personnel speak to lay people (non-medical professionals), the listener is flooded with their knowledge of medical-speak or they treat you as if you are being prepped for a remedial reading class. Some medical professionals will over-simplify, talk just a little louder in case you didn't hear them, and they speak very slowly for a few sentences, and then rush on to bury you in more jargon. Our medical professionals are very dedicated professionals who are doing the best they can and I have the highest respect for them. So, we should probably take the time to learn their a little bit of their language.

One of the most annoying things about the car business that I am involved with is the use of acronyms and jargon. We use abbreviated words all the time. I once overheard an automobile service advisor in a dealership talking to a customer on the phone. She had brought her vehicle in for service earlier that day. The conversation went like this: "Hello, Ma'am? We had the tech look at your vehicle and you will probably need to have your pads replaced, your rotors turned and, while you're here, we should R&R your calipers. By the way, has anyone ever told you that your rear main seal is leaking? And we also think the mass airflow sensor needs to be looked at. And we can have all of that ready for you by this afternoon."

I swear, that's exactly what he said. I'm sure that after she picked her jaw up off the ground, she told him she'd rather wait awhile, and how soon could she pick up her car? Just what did all of that mean? I doubt that the service advisors comments meant very much to the customer.

Jargon and acronyms are used between people as a kind of verbal shorthand to convey information. They are used frequently as a shortcut to the complexities of the English language. Every profession and job has them. In today's world, text messaging is doing the same thing on a whole new level. All of this is okay, unless you are not an insider to the knowledge base. When you are in the business of dealing with the public, as medical professionals are, jargon and acronyms should never be used when dealing with nonprofessionals.

I've visited with doctors, nurses and sources like the American Heart Association to collect a number of medical terms, jargon, and acronyms that you will see in this book. Many of them you may hear in conversations regarding a variety of heart conditions. This list is just a guide, and is not meant as a comprehensive dictionary of terms. This guide is, for the most part, a simple explanation, in layman's terms, of what some of these things mean. I hope they help.

Ablation
The word Ablation simply means elimination or removal. Ablation also refers to a procedure that eliminates extra electrical pathways within the heart that cause fast or irregular heart rhythms.

ACE Inhibitor (angiotensin-converting enzyme)
An ACE Inhibitor is a medication that opens up blood vessels, making it easier for the heart to pump blood forward to the body. ACE Inhibitors are also is used to lower blood pressure. Never play poker with a nurse who has an ACE Inhibitor up her sleeve.

Acyanotic
The word Acyanotic refers to a group of congenital heart defects, those from birth in which there is a normal amount of oxygen in the bloodstream, which gives a pink color to the lips and fingernails.

AF (Atrial Fibrillation)
AF is short for Arterial Fibrillation and is an Irregular Heart rhythm.

Anastomosis
Anastomosis is a surgical connection, often between two blood vessels.

Aneurysms
Aneurysms are small blister-like pouches on blood vessel walls. The blood vessel or area of the heart is thin or weakened at this point. They can rupture, causing bleeding.

Angina
Angina pectoris or angina is a recurring pain or discomfort in the chest. Angina happens when some part of the heart does not receive enough blood. The pain can feel like heaviness, a burning sensation or a discomfort in the left arm or jaw. Do not underrate head, arm or chest discomfort symptoms they may be more serous than you think.

Angiography
Angiography is a procedure to x-ray blood vessels. A dye is injected into the blood vessel using a catheter or small tube. The blood vessels can be seen because the dye shows up in the x-ray pictures. Blockages and other problems interfering with the flow of blood, for example in the legs, heart, or brain can be identified.

Angioplasty
Angioplasty is a method or procedure to open clogged arteries. A catheter is snaked into the narrowed coronary artery. A tiny balloon or another device is attached to the tip of the catheter. The balloon is used to stretch or break open the narrow part of the artery and improve the passage for blood flow. When this is done, the catheter is removed.

Anticoagulant
Any medication that keeps blood from clotting is referred to as an anticoagulant.

Antihypertensive
Hypertensive is another word for high blood pressure. An antihypertensive medication is one that lowers blood pressure.

Antiarrhythmic
An antiarrhythmic medication is given to treat arrhythmia or an irregular heart beat.

Antiplatelet
Antiplatelet medication reduces platelets in the blood and prevents the blood from clotting. Aspirin has been known to lower platelets in the blood.

Aorta
The aorta is the largest artery in the body and the primary blood vessel that carries oxygenated blood out of the heart to the rest of the body.

Aortic Arch
On the heart, the aortic arch is the curved portion of the aorta, the large blood vessel that carries oxygen-rich blood away from the heart to the body.

Aortic Regurgitation
Aortic regurgitation is a backwards leakage of blood from the aorta, through a weakened aortic valve, into the left ventricle. This results in stress in the left heart and an inadequate blood flow to the body.

Aortic Stenosis
Aortic stenosis is a narrowing of the opening of the aortic valve, the valve that regulates blood flow from the left ventricle into the aorta.

Aortic Valve
The aortic valve is the valve that regulates blood flow from the heart into the aorta.

Arrhythmia (Also called dysrhythmia)
Arrhythmia is a fast, slow, or irregular heartbeat.

Arterioles
Arterioles are small branches of arteries.

Artery
An artery is a blood vessel that carries oxygen rich blood away from the heart to the body. The major arteries of the heart are called the coronary arteries.

Arteriosclerosis
Arteriosclerosis is commonly called "hardening of the arteries"; a variety of conditions caused by cholesterol, fat or calcium deposits in the artery walls causing them to thicken, which cuts down the flow of oxygen-rich blood to the heart.

ASA Aspirin
ASA, which stands for acetylsalicylic acid, is the chemical compound of common aspirin. Aspirin is used as an antiplatelet in the blood.

ASD (Atrial Septal Defect)
An Arterial septal defect (ASD) is a small hole in the septum or top part of the heart.

Asplenia
Simply defined, asplenia is the absence of the spleen, either from improper development before birth, or due to the surgical removal of the spleen resulting from injury or disease.

Atrial Fibrillation (AF)
Arterial fibrillation is the very fast and irregular beating or quivering of the upper two chambers of the heart. This is what happens before arrest or as the heart stops all together.

Atrial Flutter
An arterial flutter is a description sometimes used in place of Atrial Fibrillation. Very fast beating of the atria or the upper two chambers of the heart. An arterial flutter sometimes occurs when people fall in love.

Atrial Septal Defect (ASD)
An Atrial septal defect or ASD is a hole in the wall between the right and left atria, the two upper chambers of the heart.

Atrial Septum
The wall between the right and left atria is referred to as the atrial septum. The two upper chambers of the heart are called the septum.

Atrioventricular Canal
The atrioventricular canal refers to a congenital heart, from birth, defect involving an opening low in the arterial septum or wall between the atria with an opening high in the ventricular septum, and abnormal development of the mitral and/or tricuspid valves.

Atrium (Atria Plural)
The atrium is one of two upper chambers in the heart.

Atrioventricular block
An atrioventricular block is an interruption of the electrical signal between the atria and the ventricles.

Atrioventricular (AV) node
The atrioventricular node is a cluster of cells between the atria and ventricles that regulate the electrical current.

Automatic Implantable defibrillator
Referred to in the book as an ICD, an automatic implantable defibrillator is a device used to correct serious ventricular arrhythmias that can lead to sudden death. The defibrillator is surgically placed inside the patient's chest. There an ICD monitors the heart's rhythm and quickly identifies serious arrhythmias. With an electrical shock, an ICD immediately disrupts a deadly arrhythmia. (See ICD.)

B-B Beta-Blocker
Beta blockers are medication given to control the heart rate and rhythm

Bacterial Endocarditis
Bacterial endocarditis is a bacterial infection that can affect the valves and interior surfaces of the heart.

Balloon Angioplasty
A balloon angioplasty is a procedure that is usually done in the cardiac catheterization laboratory (cath lab) that uses a catheter (tube) with a balloon in the tip to open a narrowed valve or blood vessel.

Beta-Blocker
A beta blocker is a medication that limits the activity of epinephrine, a hormone that increases blood pressure. (See B-B Beta Blocker.)

Bicuspid
In heart language a bicuspid is a valve that has two leaflets. In dental language a bicuspid is a tooth.

Biopsy
A biopsy is a procedure in which tissue samples are removed from the body for microscopic examination in order to establish a diagnosis.

Blood Clot
A blood clot is a thick, gelled mass of blood. When you form a blood clot the platelets have done their job and the blood coagulates.

Blood Pressure (BP)
Blood pressure is the force or pressure exerted by the heart against

the walls of the arteries when pumping blood and is the measurable pressure of blood in the arteries. Pressure is measured in systolic (the upper number) and diastolic (the lower number), such as 120/80, and is measured in millimeters of mercury against a meter stick.

Blood Pressure Cuff
A blood pressure cuff is a device that is usually placed around the upper portion of the arm to measure blood pressure.

BMI (Body Mass Index)
BMI is a measure of weight relative to height to determine if a person is overweight.

BNP (Brain and Peptide)
BNP is a blood enzyme which can be measured to diagnose heart failure (HF).

Brady
Brady is a suffix meaning slow.

Bradycardia
Bradycardia refers to an abnormally slow heartbeat.

Bundle-Branch Block
This is a condition in which the heart's electrical system is unable to normally conduct the electrical signal.

Bypass Surgery
In a coronary artery bypass operation, a blood vessel, usually taken from the leg or chest and is grafted onto the blocked artery, bypassing the blocked area. If more than one artery is blocked, a bypass can be done on each artery. The blood can then go around the obstruction to supply the heart with enough blood to relieve chest pain. There may be multiple bypasses grafted to supply blood.

CA (Coronary Artery)
A coronary artery is a blood vessel that supplies blood to the tissues of the heart.

CABG (Coronary Artery Bypass Grafts)
Coronary artery bypass grafts are a surgical treatment for severe heart disease. (See Bypass surgery.)

CAD (Coronary Artery Disease)
CAD or coronary artery disease is another way to describe the narrowing of the coronary arteries that supply blood to the heart.

Calcium Channel Blocker
A calcium channel blocker is another medication that lowers blood pressure.

Capillaries
Capillaries are tiny blood vessels between arteries and veins that distribute oxygen-rich blood to the body. They are so small that often only one cell passes through them at a time, in a process called capillary action.

Cardiac
The word cardiac is almost anything pertaining to the heart.

Cardiac Arrest
Simply stated, a cardiac arrest is when your heart stops.

Cardiac Catheterization
Cardiac catheterization is a diagnostic procedure in which a tiny, hollow tube (catheter) is inserted into an artery or vein in order to evaluate the heart and blood vessels.

Cardiac Enzymes
Cardiac enzymes are checked in blood tests to diagnose a heart attack.

Cardiac Output
Cardiac output is the volume or the amount of blood that goes through the circulatory system in one minute.

Cardiologist
A cardiologist is a physician who specializes in the medical evaluation and treatment of heart diseases.

Cardiology
Cardiology is the study of the heart and the clinical study and practice of treating the heart.

Cardiomyopathy
Cardiomyopathy is a disease that causes the heart muscle to weaken and lose its pumping strength.

Cardiophysiology
Cardio refers to the heart. Physiology is the science that treats the functions of the living organism and its parts, and of the physical and chemical factors and processes involved. Many cardiologists are also cardio physiologists as well. A Cardiophysiologist is a doctor who specializes in the chemistry and function of the heart.

Cardiovascular (CV)
Cardiovascular refers to the heart and blood vessel (circulatory) system.

Cardiovascular Diseases
Cardiovascular disease is any diseases of the heart and blood vessel system, such as coronary heart disease, heart attack, high blood pressure, stroke, angina (chest pain), and rheumatic heart disease.

Cardioversion
Cardioversion is the procedure of applying electrical shock to the chest to change an abnormal heartbeat into a normal one. This is what happens when an AED is used.

Carotid Artery
Carotid arteries are the two major arteries on either side of the neck that supply blood to the brain.

Catheter
A catheter is a small, thin tube used during a cardiac catheterization procedure to inject dye, obtain blood samples, and measure pressures inside the heart. A catheter may also refer to a small tube used to help drain the bladder during and after a surgical procedure.

Catheterization
Catherization is a test used to explore the coronary arteries, using a fine tube (catheter) that's put into an artery or vein of an arm or leg and passed into the arteries of the heart. This can be used in the diagnosis of heart disease.

CCU (Coronary Care Unit)
The CCC ward is where heart emergencies are treated.

Cholesterol
Cholesterol is best described as waxy substance that is produced by the human body. Cholesterol is also found in animal fats, shellfish, and in dairy products (such as beef, chicken, pork, butter, milk, cheese, and eggs). The body needs cholesterol to produce hormones. When too much cholesterol circulates in the blood, atherosclerosis (hardening of the arteries) and an increased risk of heart disease may result.

Cineangiography
Cineangiography is the procedure of taking moving pictures to show the passage of dye through blood vessels. Cine is the prefix meaning movies, like in cinema.

Circulatory System
Circulatory pertains to the heart and blood vessels, and the circulation of blood. The circulatory system is also called the cardiovascular system.

Closed Heart Surgery
Closed heart surgery is an operation that repairs problems involving the blood vessels attached to the heart, and may not need the use of the heart-lung bypass machine.

Coarctation of the Aorta
Coarctation of the aorta is a congenital heart defect that results in narrowing of the aorta.

Collateral Vessels
Collateral vessels are new blood vessels that are created by the body to provide extra blood flow to an area when the blood vessel(s) there are already are too small, narrowed, or blocked.

Computerized Tomography Scan (Also called CT or CAT scan)
A CAT scan is a non-invasive procedure that takes cross-sectional images of the brain or other internal organs; to detect any abnormalities that may not show up on an ordinary x-ray. Often they are presented in color.

Conduction System
Conduction system is the electrical system inside the heart that stimulates the heart to beat.

Congenital
Congenital simply means present at birth.

Congenital Heart Defect
A congenital heart defect is a heart problem present at birth, caused by improper development of the heart during fetal development.

Congenital Heart Disease
See congenital heart defect.

Congestive Heart Failure (CHF)
Congestive heart failure is a condition in which the heart cannot pump out all of the blood. This can lead to an accumulation of blood in the vessels going into the heart and an accumulation of fluid in the body tissues. Excess blood in the pulmonary or lungs blood vessels can also occur, leading to fluid accumulation in the lungs which creates the congestion.

Coronary Arteries
Coronary arteries are the two arteries that come from the aorta to provide blood to the heart muscle.

Coronary Heart Disease (CHD)
Coronary heart disease is the most common form of heart disease. This type of heart disease is caused by a narrowing of the coronary arteries that feed the heart, which results in not-enough oxygen-rich blood reaching the heart.

CVD (Cardiovascular Disease)
Disease affecting the heart and its circulation is referred to a Cardiovascular Disease or CVD for short.

CVP (Central Venous Pressure)
CVP or central venous pressure is a measure of the pressure in the internal blood vessels of the body.

CVS (Cardiovascular System)
CVS is the abbreviation for cardiovascular system which is the heart and all of the blood vessels in the body, also known as the circulatory system.

Cyanosis & Cyanotic
Cyanosis is due to an insufficient oxygen supply in the blood that would leave tissue appearing blue. Cyan is the color blue. Blue babies are born cyanotic.

Defibrillator
A defibrillator is an electronic device used to deliver an electronic shock to establish a normal heartbeat. This is not to be confused with a de-fib-a-lator, which is the lariat of truth that Wonder Woman often uses to detect lies.

Dextrocardia
Dextrocdardia is a heart that is "flipped over," so that the structures that are normally on the right side of the chest are on the left, and vice versa. The arteries and veins are connected correctly. This occurs due to an abnormality in heart development during pregnancy.

Diastole
Diastole is the time during each heartbeat when the ventricles are at rest, filling with blood and not pumping.

Diastolic Blood Pressure
Diastolic is the lowest blood pressure measure in the arteries, which occurs between heartbeats when the heart is at rest.

Diuretic
A diuretic medication is one that helps the kidneys to remove excess fluids from the body, lowering blood pressure as well as decreasing edema (swelling).

Doppler Ultrasound
Doppler ultrasound is a procedure that uses sound waves to evaluate heart, blood vessels, and valves.

Double Outlet Right Ventricle
A double outlet right ventricle is a congenital heart defect in which both the aorta and the pulmonary artery are connected to the right ventricle.

Down Syndrome (Also called Trisomy 21)
Down syndrome is a combination of birth defects caused by the presence of an extra #21 chromosome in each cell of the body. Many children with Down syndrome also have congenital heart disease—usually atrioventricular canal defect.

Ductus Arteriosus
The ductus arteriosus is a connection between the aorta and the pulmonary artery that is necessary in fetal life, but becomes unnecessary after birth.

Dyspnea
Simply stated, dyspnea is a shortness of breath.

Dysrhythmia
Dysrhythmia is an abnormal heart rhythm.

Ebstein's Anomaly
Ebstein's anomaly is an abnormal development of the tricuspid valve during pregnancy, causing an abnormally positioned valve that does not open easily (stenosis) and allows backflow of blood from the right ventricle into the right atrium (regurgitation).

Echo (Echocardiogram or Echocardiography)
An echocardiogram is an ultrasound that evaluates the structure and function of the heart by using sound waves recorded on an electronic sensor that produces a moving picture of the heart and heart valves. This is the same process used by pregnant women to view the fetus before birth.

ECU (Eternal Care Unit)
The ECU is a slang term for death. All Sudden Cardiac Arrest survivors have been to the ECU.

Edema
An edema is a swelling.

Effusion
Effusion is a gathering or a collection of fluid in a closed cavity.

Ejection Fraction (EF)
EF or Ejection Fraction is the measurement of the amount of blood pumped out of the ventricles. When the left ventricle of your heart contracts blood is forced into the veins and pushes blood throughout the body. This is the ventricle that does the work pushing the blood into the arteries. The heart literally ejects the blood out of this left ventricle. Not all of the blood is ejected from this ventricle each contraction. The percentage that is ejected is measured between each heartbeat in a fraction called the ejection fraction. 55% to 60% is considered a good ejection fraction. When the percentage falls below 55%, your heart is not forcing as much blood as needed into your arteries. The left ventricle is the number we look at for a measurement but the right can be measured as well. When your EF falls below 35% your heart is working too hard, and work needs to be done to get your number up.

142

Electrocardiogram (ECG or EKG)
The EKG is a test that records the electrical activity of the heart, shows abnormal rhythms such as arrhythmias or dysrhythmias and detects heart muscle stress.

Electron Beam Computed Tomography (EBCT)
The EBCT is a test to identify and measure calcium buildup in and around the coronary arteries. Calcium build-ups can indicate an increased risk of heart disease.

Electrophysiological Study (EPS)
An EPS study is a cardiac catheterization to study electrical current in patients who have arrhythmias.

Embolism
An embolism is a clot in a blood vessel.

Endocardium
The endocardium is the membrane that covers the inside surface of the heart.

Endocarditis
Endocarditis is a bacterial infection that can form on the valves and on interior surfaces of the heart.

Enlarged Heart
An enlarged heart is condition of the heart in which is larger than normal.

EP Studies (Electrophysiological studies)
EP studies are a detailed look at heart rhythm.

ETT (Electrocardiogram Treadmill Test)
An ETT test is a recording of the heartbeat and rhythm while walking on a treadmill.

Epicardium
The epicardium is the membrane that covers the outside of the heart.

Exercise Electrocardiogram (ECG or EKG)
An exercise EKG is a test to assess the cardiac rhythm and function by having the patient exercise on a treadmill or bicycle.

Failure to Thrive

Failure to thrive is a phrase defined as a failure to grow and gain weight, often due to increased energy expenditure with congenital heart disease.

Fat

Fat is one of the nutrients that supplies calories to the body. The body needs only small amounts of fat. Foods contain different types of fat. Saturated fat, for example, is found in greatest amounts in food from animals such as butter, cheese, milk and ice cream, as well as meat and poultry skin. A few vegetable fats such as coconut oil, cocoa butter, palm kernel oil and palm oil are also high in saturated fats.

Fibric Acid Derivatives

Fibric Acid Derivatives are a type of cholesterol lowering drug.

Fibrillation

Fibrillation can best be described as rapid contractions of the heart muscles, sometimes called a quivering of the heart muscle. When your heart is in fibrillation blood cannot be pumped in or out properly. Fibrillation can lead to cardiac arrest, where the heart simply stops functioning.

Fluoroscopy

Flouroscopy is an X-ray procedure that takes continuous pictures to evaluate moving structures within the body, such as the heart.

Flutter

Flutter is defined as ineffective contractions of the heart muscles.

Fontan Procedure

A fontan procedure is a surgical procedure performed to repair heart defects in which only one ventricle is functional. This procedure connects the right atrium to the pulmonary artery, allowing oxygen-poor (blue) blood from the body to flow into the lungs.

Foramen Ovale

A foramen ovale describes a hole between the right and left atria, present in all unborn children that will remain open after birth for variable periods of time.

Generic Drug

A generic drug is a medicine that has the same active ingredient as a trademarked brand-named version. Generic drugs usually cost less than their brand-named versions.

Glenn Shunt
A Glenn shunt is a surgical connection between the superior vena cava and the right pulmonary artery, allowing oxygen-poor (blue) blood to flow into the lungs.

Heart Attack (Also called Myocardial Infarction)
A heart attack occurs when one of more regions of the heart muscle experience a severe or prolonged decrease in oxygen supply caused by a blocked blood flow to the heart muscle.

HB (Heart Block)
HB is an abbreviation for heart block or an interruption of the electrical pathway causing a slowing of the heart rate.

Heart Failure (CHF)
CHF is also called congestive heart failure. This is a serious condition in which the heart is unable to pump enough blood to supply the body's needs. CHF occurs when excess fluid starts to leak into the lungs, causing breathing difficulty, fatigue and weakness, and sleeping problems. High blood pressure is the number one risk factor for CHF.

Heart-Lung Bypass Machine
A heart and lung bypass machine is one that performs the heart and lung function during open-heart surgery.

Heart Rhythm
Heart rhythm is a heartbeat in a regular rhythm.

Heart Transplant
A heart transplant is an operation in which a diseased heart is replaced with a healthy heart from a donor.

Heart Valve Prolapse
A heart valve prolapse is a condition of the heart valve is partially open instead of being closed.

High Blood Pressure HBP, (Also called Hypertension)
High blood pressure or HBP is pressure in the blood vessels that is above the normal range (See Blood Pressure.)

High-Density Lipoprotein (HDL)
HDL is the "good" cholesterol that promotes breakdown and removal of cholesterol from the body.

Holter Monitor
A Holter monitor is a portable EKG machine worn for a twenty-four-hour period or longer to evaluate irregular, fast, or slow heart rhythms while engaging in normal activities.

Homograft
A homograft is a blood vessel taken from a tissue donor; used to replace a defective blood vessel, most often the pulmonary artery or aorta.

Hypertension
Hypertension is the medical term for high blood pressure. Readings of 140/90 or higher are considered high.

Hypertrophic Obstructive Cardiomyopathy (Also called HOCM, Hypertrophic Cardiomyopathy, Asymmetrical Septal Hypertrophy (ASH), or Idiopathic Hypertrophic Subaortic Stenosis (IHSS).)
Basically, HOCM is an enlarged heart muscle that causes impeded blood flow.

Hypoplastic
Hypoplastic refers to an abnormally small organ or blood vessel due to abnormal development prior to birth. Hypoplastic left heart syndrome is a congenital heart defect in which the left side of the heart is poorly developed, resulting in small mitral valve, left ventricle, and aorta.

Hypotension
Hypotension is low blood pressure.

Hypoxia
Hypoxia is an abnormal oxygen content in the organs and tissues of the body.

ICD (Implantable Cardioverter Defibrillator)
An electronic device surgically implanted in the chest with leads to the heart to monitor heart rhythm and detect ventricular fibrillation. When ventricular fibrillation occurs, the device will deliver a shock to restore rhythm. An ICD is sometimes called an Implantable Cardio Defibrillator and may also be called an Internal Cardio Defibrillator. What ever you call them, they save lives.

ICU (Intensive Care Unit)
The ICU is the ward of the hospital where patients are constantly monitored for potential emergencies.

IHD (Ischaemic Heart Disease)
IHD is an abbreviation used to describe the narrowing of the coronary arteries that supply blood to the heart.

Immunosuppressive Medications
Immunosuppressive medications are medications that suppress the body's immune system and are used to minimize rejection of transplanted organs.

Incision
An incision is a cut made with a surgical instrument during an operation.

Infarct
An infarct is the area of the heart tissue damaged by a lack of blood and oxygen.

Inferior Vena Cava
Inferior vena cava is the large blood vessel (vein) that returns blood from the legs and abdomen to the heart. This vein is sometimes used in bypass surgery.

Insufficiency
A valve deformity that allows the blood to leak backwards when the valve is closed is referred to as insufficiency.

Ischemia
Ischemia is a decreased flow of oxygenated blood to an organ due to obstruction in an artery. Ischemic is the state of not having enough blood flow.

Jugular Veins
Jugular veins carry blood from the head back to the heart.

Kawasaki Disease
Kawasaki disease is an immune system disorder affecting the heart, particularly the coronary arteries. The term has nothing to do with motorcycles and guys who want them.

Left Atrium
The left atrium is the upper left-hand chamber of the heart which receives oxygen-rich (red) blood from the lungs via the four pulmonary veins, and then sends this blood to the left ventricle. This is the workhorse ventricle of the heart.

Left Ventricle
The left ventricle is the lower left-hand chamber of the heart which receives oxygen-rich (red) blood from the left atrium that is pumped into the aorta, which then takes the blood to the body. The left ventricle must be strong and muscular in order to pump enough blood to the body.

Lesion
A lesion is a cut, injury or wound.

Lipid
The word lipid is simply any fatty substance in the blood, including cholesterol and triglycerides.

Lipoproteins
Lipoprotines are transporters of fatty substances in the blood.

Low-Density Lipoprotein (LDL)
LDL is the primary cholesterol-carrying substance in the body. In large amounts LDL accumulates inside arteries and can lead to cardiovascular disease.

Lumen
Lumen is the hollow area inside of a blood vessel.

Magnetic Resonance Imaging (MRI)
An MRI is a diagnostic procedure that uses a combination of large magnets, radio frequencies, and a computer to produce detailed images of organs and structures within the body.

Marfan Syndrome
Marfan syndrome is a genetic disorder that affects the connective tissue of the body. This syndrome causes dilation of blood vessels and abnormalities of cardiac valves.

Mechanical Valve
A mechanical valve is an artificial valve used to replace a diseased or defective valve, most often the aortic valve.

Median Sternotomy

A median sternotomy is an incision in the center of the chest, from the top to the bottom of the breastbone or sternum, used for many congenital heart defect repair surgeries.

MI (Myocardial Infarction)

MI is an abbreviation for a heart attack.

Mitral Valve

Mitral valve is the valve that controls blood flow between the left atrium and left ventricle in the heart.

Mitral Valve Prolapse

A mitral valve prolapse is an abnormality of the valve between the left atrium and left ventricle of the heart that causes backward flow of blood from the left ventricle into the left atrium.

mmHg

mmHg is an abbreviation for millimeters of mercury (Hg). The measurement is used to express measures of blood pressure against a meter stick.

Monounsaturated Fats

Monounsaturated fats are dietary fats, such as olive oil or canola oil, which may lower LDL cholesterol levels. Look for foods that are high in Monounsaturated fats.

Murmur

A murmur is a blowing or rasping sound heard while listening to the heart that may or may not indicate problems within the heart or circulatory system.

Myocardial Infarction (Also called Heart Attack)

A myocardial infarction occurs when one of more regions of the heart muscle experiences a severe or prolonged decrease in oxygen supply caused by a blocked blood flow to the heart muscle, which causes the heart to stop.

Myocardium

Myocardium is another word for the heart muscle.

Myocardial ischemia

A myocardial ischemia is an insufficient blood flow to part of the heart.

Myocarditis
Myocarditis is an inflammation of the heart muscles. The suffix "its" is" is simply 'the condition of.'

Myocardium
The myocardium describes the muscular layer of the heart.

Noninvasive Procedure
A noninvasive procedure is a diagnostic effort or treatment that does not require entering the body or puncturing the skin.

Obesity
Obesity is defined as being overweight by 30% of the ideal body weight.

Occluded Artery
An occluded artery is an artery that is narrowed by plaque, impeding the flow of blood.

Open-heart Surgery
Open heart surgery is a procedure that involves opening the chest and heart while a heart-lung machine performs for the heart and lungs during the operation.

Oxygen Desaturation
Oxygen desaturation refers to insufficient amounts of oxygen in the bloodstream. Desaturation can occur when oxygen-poor (blue) blood from the right side of the heart circulation mixes with oxygen-rich (red) blood in the left side of the heart circulation and goes to the body. Normal oxygen saturation in the arteries is 95% to 100%.

Oxygen Saturation
Oxygen saturation is the extent to which hemoglobin is saturated with oxygen (Hemoglobin is an element in the bloodstream that binds with oxygen that is carried to the organs and tissues of the body.) A normal oxygen saturation of the blood leaving the heart to the body is 95% to 100%. The oxygen saturation of the blood returning to the heart after delivering oxygen to the body is 75%.

Pacemaker
A pacemaker is an electronic device that is surgically placed in the patient's body and connected to the heart to regulate the heartbeat. In

some cases, ICD's and Pacemakers have both been implanted in heart patients to monitor and regulate a heart beat.

Palpitation
Palpitation is a sensation in the chest caused by an irregular heartbeat. Palpitations can be small bursts of a fast heart rhythm.

Patent
Patent is a word that simply means open.

Patent Ductus Arteriosus (PDA)
A PDA is a blood vessel present in all infants that usually closes shortly after birth. These vessels connect the aorta to the pulmonary artery. When open, extra blood is allowed to pass through from the aorta to the lungs.

Patent Foramen Ovale
A patent foramen ovale is an opening in the arterial septum (wall between the right and left atria) that is present in all infants, but which usually closes shortly after birth. When open, extra blood is allowed to pass through the opening from the left atrium to the right atrium.

Pericardial Effusion
Paricardial effusion is a build up of excess fluid between the heart and the membrane that surrounds the heart, which is often due to inflammation.

Pericarditis
Pericardis is an inflammation or infection of the sac that surrounds the heart.

Pericardiocentesis
Pericardiocentesis is a diagnostic procedure that uses a needle to draw fluid from the pericardium.

Pericardium
The pericardium is the membrane that surrounds the heart and is called the pericardial sac.

Plaque
Plaque is deposits of fat or other substances attached to the artery wall.

Platelets
Platelets are cells found in the blood that assist in clotting.

Polyunsaturated Fat
Polyunsaturated fat is a type of fat found in vegetable oils and margarines that does not appear to raise blood cholesterol levels. Food labels will often describe if polyunsaturated fats are present.

Post-Pericardiotomy Syndrome
Post pericardiotomy syndrome describes a condition where there is a build up of excess fluid between the heart and the membrane that surrounds the heart and is often due to inflammation after open-heart surgery. ("Post" means after, and "pericardiotomy" means opening the membrane around the heart for open-heart surgery.)

Premature Arterial Contraction (PAC)
A PAC is an early heartbeat started by the atria.

Premature Ventricular Contraction (PVC)
A PVC in medicine refers to an early heartbeat started by the ventricles.

Prophylaxis
Prophylaxis simply means prevention.

Prostaglandin E1
Prostaglandin E1 is an intravenous medication used to keep a patents ductus arteriosus from closing and preserve blood flow to the lungs.

PTCA (Percutaneous Transluminal Coronary Angioplasty)
PTCA is a procedure performed to open clogged arteries. A catheter is positioned in the narrowed coronary artery and a small balloon is inflated and deflated to stretch or break open the narrowing and improve the passage for blood flow.

Pulmonary
Pulmonary is a term pertaining to the lungs and respiratory system; the Pulmonary System.

Pulmonary Artery
The pulmonary artery is the blood vessel connecting the right ventricle to the lungs, allowing oxygen-poor (blue) blood to receive oxygen.

Pulmonary Edema
Pulmonary edema is a condition in which there is fluid accumulation in the lungs caused by an incorrectly functioning heart.

Pulmonary Valve
The pulmonary valve is the heart valve located between the right ventricle and the pulmonary artery that controls blood flow to the lungs.

Pulmonary Vein
The vessel that carries oxygenated blood from the lungs to the left side of the heart is called the pulmonary vein.

Pulse Oximeter
A pulse oximeter is a device that measures the amount of oxygen in the blood. Normal oxygen saturation in the arteries is 95% to 100%.

Radioisotope
A radioisotope is a radioactive material injected into the body so a nuclear scanner can make pictures.

Regurgitation
Regurgitation is the backward flow of fluid. In the heart regurgitation can be the backward flow of blood caused by a defective heart valve.

Renal
The word renal refers to the kidneys and kidney function.

Rheumatic Fever
Rheumatic fever is a disease caused by a strep infection that may damage the heart valves.

Right Atrium
The right atrium is the upper right chamber of the heart, which receives oxygen-poor (blue) blood from the body and sends this blood to the right ventricle.

Right Ventricle
The right ventricle is the lower right chamber of the heart, which receives oxygen-poor (blue) blood from the right atrium and sends this blood to the pulmonary artery.

Risk Factor
Risk factor is defined as a condition, element, or activity that may

adversely affect the heart. Controllable risk factors include cigarette smoking, high blood pressure, high blood cholesterol, obesity, excessive alcohol use, drug use and abuse of dietary supplements. Non-controllable risk factors include age and gender and genetics.

Ross Procedure
A Ross procedure is a surgical procedure performed to repair aortic stenosis; the child's own pulmonary valve and base of the pulmonary artery (autograft) replace the defective aorta, while a homograft (blood vessel from a tissue donor) replaces the pulmonary valve and base of the pulmonary artery.

Rubella
Rubella is an illness that can cause birth defects, including congenital heart disease if a woman contracts this condition for the first time during pregnancy; can be prevented by immunization with the MMR (measles) vaccine.

Saturated Fat
Saturated fat is fat that is found in foods from animal meats and skin, dairy products, and some vegetables. Saturated fats are usually solid at room temperatures and can increase LDL levels.

Septal Defect
A septal defect is a hole in the wall between the atria or the ventricles (upper or lower heart chambers).

Septum
The septum is a muscle wall between the atria or ventricles (upper or lower heart chambers).

Shunt
A shunt is a connector to allow blood flow between two locations.

Sinus Node
Sinus nodes are the cells that produce the electrical impulses that cause the heart to contract.

Sinus Rhythm
Sinus rhythm is a normal heart rhythm in which each heartbeat originates in the sinus node, and proceeds through the rest of the electrical conduction system normally.

Sinus Tachycardia
Sinus tachycardia is a heart rhythm that originates in the sinus node and proceeds through the rest of the electrical conduction system, but is faster than normal.

Sodium
Sodium is also called salt, a mineral that can contribute to high blood pressure.

Sphygmomanometer
A sphygmomanometer is an instrument used to measure blood pressure.

Statins
Statins are a type of cholesterol-lowering drug that keeps the liver from producing as much cholesterol and helps the liver remove cholesterol out of the blood stream.

Stent
A stent is a wire mesh tube inserted into arteries to help keep them open. Stents can be drug coated or non-drug coated and they look like a small tubular chain link fence.

Stenosis
Stenosis is a narrowing or constriction of a blood vessel or valve in the heart.

Stethoscope
A stethoscope is an instrument used to listen to the heart and other sounds in the body. You can always identify the doctors because they are wearing one.

Sternotomy
Sternotomy is a surgical incision made in the breastbone at or near the sternum.

Sternum
The breastbone is also called the sternum.

Stress
Stress is defined as mental or physical tension that results from physical, emotional, or chemical causes.

Stress Test
Stress tests are the treadmill test used to record the heart rhythm during extreme exercise. These tests in conjunction with a cardio echo reading can determine the ejection fraction.

Stroke
Stroke is the sudden disruption of blood flow to the brain. Many strokes are caused by a clot of blood traveling into the brain (thrombosis). A stroke may also be caused by a rupture of a blood vessel (hemorrhage).

Subclavian
The subclavian vein is a blood vessel that branches from the aorta and takes oxygen-rich (red) blood to the head and arms.

Subclavian Flap
The subclavian flap is a surgical procedure performed to repair coarctation of the aorta, using part of the left subclavian artery as a patch to enlarge a narrowed aorta.

Superior Vena Cava
The superior vena cava is the large vein that returns blood to the heart from the head and arms.

Supraventricular Tachycardia
Supraventricular tachycardia is a fast heart rate that originates in the aorta, but does not start in the sinus node.

Syncope
Syncope is described as light-headedness or fainting caused by insufficient blood supply to the brain.

Systole
Systole is the time during the heartbeat when the ventricles are pumping blood, either to the lungs or to the body.

Systolic Blood Pressure
Systolic blood pressure is the highest blood pressure measured in the arteries in millimeters against a meter stick.

Tachycardia
Tachycardia is a rapid heartbeat.

Tachypnea
Tachypena is rapid breathing.

Tamponade
Tamponade is an emergency situation that occurs when blood or fluid fills the pericardial sac surrounding the heart, preventing the heart from beating effectively.

Telemetry Unit
A telemetry unit is a transmitting device. A small box with wires attached to EKG patches on the chest; used to send information about the heart-beat via radio transmission to healthcare professionals for evaluation also use a telemetry unit.

Tetralogy of Fallot (TOF)
Tetralogy of Fallot or TOF is a group of congenital heart defects, including a ventricular septal defect, obstruction to blood flow out of the right ventricle to the lungs, and an aorta that is shifted to the right. Enlargement of the right ventricle occurs as the right ventricle copes with obstruction to blood flow.

Thrombolysis
Thromoblysis is a clot-busting drug used to dissolve a blood clot that is causing a heart attack.

Thrombosis
Blockage of a blood vessel due to a blood clot is called Thromobsis.

Thoracotomy
Thoracotomy is an incision made on the right or left side of the chest between the ribs, in order to access the heart or lungs during surgery.

Trans Fat
This is vegetable oil that has been treated with hydrogen in order to make the oil more solid and provide a longer shelf life. Read food labels!

Transesophageal Echocardiography (TEE)
A TEE is a diagnostic test that uses a long tube guided into the mouth, throat, and esophagus to evaluate the structures inside the heart with sound waves.

Transplantation
Transplantation is replacing a damaged organ with one from a donor.

Transposition of the Great Arteries (Also called Transposition of the Great Vessels)
Transposition of the great arteries is a congenital heart defect involving abnormal development of the great arteries (the aorta and the pulmonary artery) during the time the heart is forming prior to birth. The aorta ends up being connected to the right ventricle, and the pulmonary artery is connected to the left ventricle, which is the opposite of the way they are normally connected.

Tricuspid Atresia
Tricuspid atresia is a congenital heart defect in which the tricuspid valve and right ventricle do not develop properly, preventing oxygen-poor (blue) blood from reaching the lungs via its normal pathway.

Tricuspid Valve
Tricuspid valve is the heart valve that controls blood flow from the right atrium into the right ventricle.

Triglyceride
Triglycerides are fats or lipids from fatty foods that are primarily found in the blood.

Trisomy 21 (Also called Down Syndrome)
Trisomy 21 is the presence of three #21 chromosomes in each cell of the body, rather than the usual pair, which causes the features otherwise known as Down syndrome. Many children with Down syndrome also have congenital heart disease-usually atrioventricular canal defect.

Truncus Arteriosus
Truncus arteriosus is a congenital heart defect involving incomplete separation of the great arteries (the aorta and the pulmonary artery) during the time the heart is forming prior to birth.

Ultrasound
An ultrasound diagnostic tool is used to evaluate organs and structures inside the body with high-frequency sound waves.

Valves
Valves are the doors between the chambers of the heart that allow blood to move forward and prevent the blood from moving backward.

The heart valves are called tricuspid, pulmonic, mitral, and aortic.

Valvuloplasty
Valvuloplasty is a procedure to repair a heart valve.

Vascular
Vascular refers to blood vessels.

Vasodilator
Vasodilator is a medication that dilates or widens the opening in a blood vessel.

Vasopressor
Vasopressor is a medication that raises blood pressure.

Vasovagal syndrome
Vasovagal syndrome is a sudden drop in blood pressure, with or without a decrease in heart rate, which is caused by a dysfunction of the nerves controlling the heart and blood vessels.

Vein
A vein is a blood vessel that carries low oxygen blood from the body back into the heart.

Ventricle
A ventricle is one of the two lower chambers of the heart.

Ventricular Fibrillation (VF)
Ventricular fibrillation or VF is a condition in which the ventricles contract in rapid and unsynchronized rhythms, sometimes quivering, and cannot pump blood into the body.

Ventricular Septal Defect (VSD)
Ventricular septal defect is an abnormal opening in the wall between the right and left ventricles.

Ventricular Tachycardia (VT)
Ventricular tachycardia is a condition in which the ventricles beat very quickly.

Vertigo
Vertigo is dizziness or the feeling that you are falling or watching the world go round.

Wolff-Parkinson-White Syndrome
Wolff Parkinson White syndrome is an extra electrical pathway that connects the atria and ventricles and causes rapid heartbeat.

X-ray
An X-ray is a diagnostic test that uses invisible electromagnetic energy beams to produce images of internal tissues, bones, and organs onto film.

15

Happy Re-Birthday!

I have recently had my second re-birthday. In other words, I am reflecting on the time that has passed since I had a Sudden Cardiac Arrest and died on an airplane. Those of us who have managed to survive this trauma refer to the anniversary of their event as a re-birthday. A re-birthday is a celebration of the day we died and returned to walk among the living again.

I know survivors who enjoy the day with a birthday cake and they surround themselves with family and friends. In many ways, I experienced a miracle to have died and be returned to your loved ones. A re-birthday is a day worthy of joy and happiness as a special day. This day is also a day to remember the other 94% of people who suffered a Sudden Cardiac Arrest and who do not return to their families and friends. They died and did not return.

So much can be done to improve the survival rate. In Minnesota, where survival is a passion, they have improved the survival rate by 300% over the death rate five years ago. There are some wonderful leaders in Minnesota communities who have taken responsibility to make sure that their communities are aware of what must be done in an emergency. Seattle and the Pacific Northwest have made great strides to improve survival rates in their part of the country. If, as a nation, we could just improve that death rate to say, 80%, that would be roughly 80,000 survivors a year instead of 24,000. This could be someone you know or even you. Every local community in the United States and countries around the world are very capable of doing this.

Sudden Cardiac Arrest is not a heart attack but a heart attack can bring on a Sudden Cardiac Arrest. Every survivor's story involves an intervention by another person. Unfortunately, many people are alone when they have a Sudden Cardiac Arrest and there is no one to provide CPR or attach the leads of an AED. That is why the numbers are so high. When people are present, many times, they do not know what to do. They do not know what they are witnessing and the person having the cardiac arrest simply is not revived. A more informed public can respond quicker and bring the necessary help faster. They can perform conventional CPR or rapid compression CPR like Call and Pump until help arrives.

During my re-birthday, I am also thinking about the many children who carry genetic markers for heart conditions, as yet undetected. Companies like Familion have tests that can be run that will determine if a person is at risk of having a treatable heart ailment. Doctors are able to test for cardiac channelopathies, which are genetically linked conditions. Testing is critical for detecting conditions such as hydrotropic myocardial heart defects. Parents should take the proactive step to have the testing performed when the test is recommended by a doctor. This simple step is absolutely critical to saving the lives of our young people as they begin to participate in athletic events. I am told that testing of parents who have cardiac channelopathies in their genetic make-up could also help to prevent some Sudden Infant Death Syndrome (SIDS) deaths. Everything must be done to stop the needless dying of our young people.

On this anniversary of my re-birth I am thinking of the other survivors and their stories. I celebrate their chance to share a few more treasured moments on this earth, to enrich others with their presence. On this day I also morn the loss of those many souls, who if only someone had been present at the right time, they might be with us today. I raise my imaginary toast to you the reader and the opportunity that lies before you to change the way things are. You have the unique potential to save the lives of many fellow human beings, simply by your acts of kindness and understanding, to educate other people about Sudden Cardiac death and what can be done to prevent this senseless method of death. Today is not too late to get started.

Patrick W. Emmett	asecondchance.book@sbcglobal.net
Heart of America Sudden Cardiac Arrest Survivors Network	www. hoascasurvivor.org
Kansas and Missouri Affiliate of the Sudden Cardiac Arrest Association	?

References, websites and sources of good information

Abbott Northwestern Hospital	www.abbottnorthwestern.com
Allina Hospitals	www.allina.com
American Heart Association	www.americanheart.org
American Heart Association Circulation	www.circulationha.org
American Heart Association Journals	www.circ.ahajounals.org
Boston Scientific/Cardiac Rhythm Management, ICD Manufacturer	www.cardiacscience.com
Brainmac – Fitness webpage	www.brainmac.com
Call and Pump	www.callandpump.com
Cardiac Science – Heart Monitoring equipment	www.cardiacscience.com
Chain of Survival	www.charinofsuvival.com
Cincinnati Children's Hospital	www.cincinnatichildrens.org
Elsevier Public Safety	www.elsiever.com
Heart Help Resource Center	www.hearthelp.com
Heart of America Sudden Cardiac Arrest Survivor Network	www.hoascasurvivor.org
Heart Rhythm Society	www.HRSonline.org

Kansas University Medical Center	www.kumc.edu
Medtronic, Inc. (Medical Equipment and AED Manufacturer)	www.medtronic.com
National Conference of State Legislatures (type in AED for keywords)	www.ncsl.org
National Society of Genetic Counselors	www.nsgc.org
PGxHealth	www.pgxhealth.com
Phillips Medical Corporation (AED Manufacturer)	www.medical.phillips.com
Tamon Brugada Senior Foundation	www.brugada.org
St. Francis Hospital System	www.stfrancis.com
St. Jude Medical	www.sjm.com
St. Luke's Hospital, KCMO	www.stlukeshealthsystem.org
Sudden Arrhythmia Death Syndromes Foundation	www.sads.org
Sudden Cardiac Arrest Association	www.suddencardiacarrest.org
Sudden Cardiac Arrest Foundation	www.sca-aware.org
University of Kansas Hospital	www.kumed.com
Welch Allyn (Medical Supplier)	www.welchallyn.com
Wilderness Survival	www.wilderness-survival.net
Zoll Medical Corp (AED Manufacturer)	www.zoll.com

The painting, Early Morning Walk was painted by Linda Wonder of Raymore, Missouri for placement in my book. Linda is a local Kansas City artist who paints dogs and horses mostly. She responded to my request for one of her pictures in my book. I am ever grateful, Linda.